P9-DER-426

THE NEUROTIC'S GUIDE TO GOD & LOVE

Dr. Lance Moore

BARBOUR
PUBLISHING

Cover image © design by DogEared Design, llc.

The author is represented by Alive Communications, Inc., 7680 Goddard Street, Suite 200, Colorado Springs CO 80920.

Published by Barbour Publishing, Inc., P.O. Box 719, Uhrichsville, Ohio 44683 www.barbourbooks.com

Our mission is to publish and distribute inspirational products offering exceptional value and biblical encouragement to the masses.

ecpa Member of the
Evangelical Christian
Publishers Association

Printed in the United States of America.
5 4 3 2 1

In loving memory of
Vivian Jensen Moore,
who loved me more than I knew

Thanks to:
Lee Hough and Alive Communication;
Shannon Hill, Paul Muckley, and Dave Lindstedt
for editorial suggestions;
the rest of the Barbour Books team for
art, production, and marketing;
Diana Moore and Dolores Teem for proofreading.

Contents

MISTAKE NUMBER ONE

"I DON'T DESERVE GRACE AND LOVE"

Mistake Number One
"I Don't Deserve Grace and Love"

Blues artist B.B. King once sang, "Nobody loves me but my mother. . .and she could be jiving, too!" If you've ever felt that way, this book is for you. Are you able to find the dark cloud in every silver lining? When something good happens to you, do you feel guilty about celebrating it? Do you peer over the shoulder of Good Fortune—sure that something awful must soon come your way in order for the cosmic scales to balance out?

Jacob Crankmeister was a pessimist's pessimist. He saw a glass neither half full nor half empty; he just saw contaminated water! When he was ten, he caught his first sight of an automobile and said, "What a noisy contraption. Those will never catch on. . .and if they do, I'll probably get run over by one." When he was twenty-five, Jacob read of how the Nazis had swarmed over Europe and sighed, "We might as well surrender; Hitler will soon rule the world." Jacob was drafted and resigned himself to dying on the battlefield. He came back without a scar. When he was forty, he witnessed prosperity and great medical advances all around him, and Mr. Crankmeister decided that fluoride and penicillin were part of a communist plot.

"There's fluoride in my water? Well, I won't last to see fifty!" When he turned a healthy fifty and the TV warned of the Cuban Missile Crisis, he built a bomb shelter, sure that nuclear Armageddon was days away. At sixty, he went to the doctor for a broken toe, and after being X-rayed, Crankmeister concluded that the radiation from the X-ray had given him terminal cancer. At the robust age of seventy, he predicted the Russians would soon conquer Europe and destroy America, but a week later, the Berlin Wall fell, and shortly thereafter the Soviet Union dissolved. Next, he read about the threat of cholesterol in bacon and eggs, which the Crankmeisters had eaten daily for breakfast, and so he made out his last will and testament, knowing he would not live to see eighty. On his eightieth birthday, he sold all his blue-chip stock because a worldwide economic depression was imminent. . .thus he missed the greatest ten-year increase of stock value in history. At eighty-eight, he reequipped his bomb shelter to prepare for the complete collapse of civilization to be caused by the Y2K bug. Finally, at ninety-five years of age, Jacob Crankmeister had a stroke. His dying words were, "See, I told you something bad was gonna happen!"

There is, of course, no one like that. . .that is, not *one* but thousands and thousands of real pessimists just like the fictitious Mr. Crankmeister. It is hard to argue with them, because bad things are indeed going to happen. But all the horrors mentioned above have been serious fears for millions of people—all for naught. The moral of this story is that worrying did not help, and even though some bad things will come our way, a lot of good things will happen, too. We have a choice about where to focus our attention, emotions, and energies.

The neurotic's greatest problem is not on the list of the actual calamities of life. Our biggest problem is our "normal" state of anxiety between the calamities. We worry about what might befall us. We experience more pain from potential and imagined catastrophes than we ever do from reality. Our dread of tomorrow poisons our joy of today.

I am a recovering neurotic. If it rained, I would blame myself. After all, a dark cloud constantly hovered over my head. I delved into philosophy, religion, and psychology, seeking the peace of mind that I would glimpse in others but never in the mirror. For many years, the more I studied my life and the world, the greater my anxieties became. Persistence paid off. I eventually found the path to freedom and joy. Now I am convinced there is an oft overlooked spiritual component to human life absolutely essential to true happiness and personal significance, which institutional religion clumsily, ham-fistedly reaches for but rarely grasps. The best theologians approach "it" with long discourses about sin, guilt, forgiveness, and grace, but they lose most of us after a few hundred pages of dry, stilted jargon. Hang with me as I try to get at this foundational truth. This chapter names our first mistaken notion to be, "I don't deserve grace and love." Technically, it is true: Saint Paul said rightly that "all have sinned and fall short of the glory of God" (Romans 3:23). We are indeed imperfect creatures who have strayed a long way from God's original design. I have done little to nothing to earn the right to God's love, and in one sense, I don't even "deserve" to live.

The psychotic, evil person does indeed need to face that fact and confess it. But for those of us I loosely call "neurotics," we already feel our failure. . .and God is waiting for us to move beyond that feeling. For us, there is a higher truth we need to claim: God has *made* us worthy of love and grace. The Christian doctrine embodied in John 3:16 is that God truly loves us and, out of that love, has come into our world and by divine sacrificial effort piled up infinite deposits of golden grace on the cosmic scale. All for us. It makes no rational sense. . .we cannot calculate the value of this God-given bullion; we cannot earn it, but it is there; and the very definition of "faith" is that we simply have to *accept* that gift and place all our shortcomings, sins, selfishness, and incompetence onto the other side of the scale.

This means two things:

1. If we don't accept this truth of unlimited grace, we are rejecting the very idea of a loving God—and we might as well jump into the dark abyss of meaningless nothingness.

2. If we do accept it, we need to rethink all our negative assumptions, lose our neurotic guilt, and cease our lifelong habit of self-defeating, self-deprecating behavior.

In the next chapter, we will discover some ways to do just that, to change our behavior by changing our understanding of God, grace, and love. There we will particularly consider the meaning of the word *love*. Here let us briefly look at the topics of grace and forgiveness.

My dear friend the Reverend Doctor Thomas Lane Butts once preached a powerful sermon about guilt and forgiveness—with a surprising result. The gist of his message was that some guilt is imaginary or driven by neuroses, and some guilt is a genuine product of our sinfulness. . .but either way, God is so full of love that we can receive unlimited forgiveness for all of it! Free of charge! (This is the definition of grace: the free gift of God's love and forgiveness. . .but even though it is free for you and me, it is not cheap grace—God paid a great price for it.) Anyway, the sermon was broadcast nationally, and a stranger from New England heard it and wrote the Alabama preacher a letter of thanks. His amazing letter went something like this:

> Dear Dr. Butts,
>
> Your words have set me free from a tremendous lifelong burden of guilt. When I was a child, I was lectured about the horrible sin of having fun on the Sabbath but rebelled against that teaching and chose to go to the theater to catch a movie on a Sunday. I committed that terrible violation of God's law on Sunday, December 7, 1941. . .that's right, the day Pearl Harbor was bombed. Ever since, I felt that I was personally

responsible for the outbreak of World War II.
As a teenager, I spent the war years picking
up scraps of metal, tin cans, and rusty nails to
donate to the scrap metal drive in support of the
war effort. . .and in a futile effort to make it up to
God. Of course I knew how irrational my feelings
were, but the guilt has stayed with me nonethe-
less. Your sermon helped me finally realize that
God could forgive me for the things I have done
wrong. . .as well as the things I didn't do wrong!

Sincerely,
John Doe

Dr. Butts wrote him back a six-word reply: "Dear Mr. Doe, You are forgiven."

That true story creates a vivid image in my mind of you and me standing before a giant cosmic scale. On one side are stacks of divine gold piled up to heaven, more than the eye can see or the hand can count, and on the other side, we are feverishly putting our meager scraps of rusted metal onto our pan of the scale, as if we could, by our own efforts, make it balance. I believe God is so loving that even if we fail to understand that the hoard of gold on the other side is there for us, God will still reach down with that hand of grace and place His thumb on our trash-heaped side of the scale to even things out for us. . .yes, even for us neurotics! That is an unexaggerated picture of divine grace.

By the way: In the name of Christ, you are forgiven.

SOLUTION NUMBER ONE

"I WILL **SWIM IN** THE SEA OF **LOVE**"

Solution Number One
"I Will Swim in the Sea of Love"

Most of us are love hungry. We are slow to admit it because we don't wish to be seen as "needy," but the truth is that we are *designed* by God to need love. The problem is that our world is imperfect and our relationships are fragmented. Even those closest to us will have moments when they say or do things that hurt us. Sometimes they abandon us entirely. Even if they don't, we *fear* they might.

When I was three years old, my mother spanked me for misbehaving. As I sat crying on the back porch steps, feeling unloved and completely alone, the neighbor's pet cat wandered over and climbed into my lap. While I petted the affectionate cat, I whined between sobs, "Kitty, you are the only one in the whole world who loves me!" (Clearly my neurotic neediness started at an early age.) Maybe you've never experienced such a day of loneliness, or a broken heart. And cows may fly.

For some people, the answer to emotional pain, alienation, and lack of love may seem as simple as finding an affectionate cat, dog, or other pet. For others, life is all about romance, so their attentions and energies are focused on finding the "perfect mate." But pets die and sweethearts sometimes turn sour. The fleeting, giddy pleasure of romantic infatuation, like a box of chocolates, will never provide real, lasting satisfaction. As Saint Augustine put it, we all have a God-shaped vacuum in our hearts and thus will be restless without God's love.

The greatest proof of God's existence is the fact that we are "hardwired" from birth with a longing to find something or someone to love and worship. This human drive explains why otherwise rational people get caught up in celebrity worship. Before becoming a minister, I was, oddly enough, a touring rock musician. From time to time, I would meet and observe big-name rock stars. Talent aside, they struck me as very ordinary people with personality flaws and insecurities that had driven them to seek stardom. Most were unhappy alcoholics or drug addicts, and not a single one I met had a healthy marriage. Yet, when they walked into a room, fans treated them with awe and reverence. Avid fans would pay any price, suffer personal discomfort, even sacrifice their virginity, for a chance to touch one of these "stars." Our worship of these miserable human gods is a twisted by-product of a good and natural inborn need and desire for the one true God.

In college, one of my professors tried to convey to our literature class how certain quintessential themes emerge again and again in popular stories and books—themes that reflect the greatest needs of our emotions and psyche. He said, "Did you see recently in the news that scientists found a way to insert a very sensitive microphone into the cardiac cavity? They determined that the heart makes a distinctive sound that, when amplified, pronounces slowly, 'Mama, mama, mama.'"

A girl in the class swallowed his tall tale hook, line, and sinker and exclaimed, "Wow! Is that really true?"

The professor laughed loudly and said, "No, it is most assuredly *not* true! I'm using a *metaphor* to describe the figurative yearning of the human heart."

Freud was probably right in asserting that adults, deep down, seek to return to the warm, secure feeling of being a child in their mama's arms. That hunger for the *maternal* reflects our *eternal* hunger—our greatest needs, the longing for lasting love, and the desire for a relationship with our original parent: God.

You probably know that God loves you and stands ready to fill the void in your soul. But knowing that in your head and experiencing it in your heart are two different things. We can't fully learn of God's love merely by academic study. Matters of the heart must be experienced by the heart. And yet correct theology is a prerequisite to full reception of divine love. False notions about God interfere with our ability to accept God's affections.

You may think of God as a harsh judge, jury, and executioner. The Bible does indeed describe God in those kinds of terms. However, we must understand that God strongly prefers *not* to relate to us in that manner. The role of judge is reserved for those who choose evil over God's love. If your intent is to do right and you have accepted God's grace and believe in the redemptive power of Christ, you should no longer think of your relationship with God in terms of a wrathful judge.

A minister friend of mine has this tongue-in-cheek sign on his office door: JESUS IS COMING. LOOK BUSY! He is poking fun at those who have a warped view of Jesus as a vengeful boss who is looking to fire His employees the first time they are caught goofing off. God is not out to get you. He is not like a traffic cop waiting with a speed trap to ticket us. He wants the best for us. Consider these promises from scripture and let them be a soothing balm for your soul:

- Jesus said, "I did not come to judge the world, but to save it" (John 12:47).

- Jesus told his disciples, "I no longer call you servants. . . . Instead, I have called you friends" (John 15:15).

- "For God did not send his Son into the world to condemn the world, but to save the world through him" (John 3:17).

- My favorite is found in 1 John 4:16: "God is love. Whoever lives in love lives in God, and God in him."

The message is clear: God doesn't want to hurt you. God loves you. Regardless of your feelings of inadequacy, or your low self-esteem, or any notions you harbor of being unloved, the truth is that the most wonderful being in the universe loves you more than you can ever imagine. Acts 17:28 announces, "'In him we live and move and have our being.'" We are swimming in a sea of God's love. Ironically, we spend most of our lives oblivious to it, like a fish in a great lake saying, "I'm thirsty!"

The Bible tells us again and again: God—who is love incarnate—permeates our existence. The more we accept and integrate that truth into our personalities, the more we fill our God-shaped vacuum. Some people view Bible study, prayer, and other spiritual duties in the negative sense of "discipline," as in a painful regimen or a punishment, as when a sergeant disciplines an unruly soldier. To the contrary, spiritual disciplines are the positive means by which we come to know more of God's love and become better connected with the divine. The more we come to know God, the more we realize that we are not alone and unloved. Religion in and of itself may not cure all of our psychological woes, but being immersed in God's love is the single most powerful tonic for neuroses.

You may have noticed that most of the biblical quotes in this chapter come from the Gospel and first Epistle of John. I offer this to you as a cure for your feelings of being unloved: Read John. Daily read the words of the man who described himself as "the disciple whom Jesus loved." I wish we knew more about the apostle John. My guess is that he was a full-fledged neurotic until he met Jesus, and then Christ saw right through John to his empty heart and began to fill it with unconditional, unlimited love. In three short chapters (1 John 2, 3, and 4), the apostle uses the word *love* more than twenty times. It was John who recorded these famous words: "For God so loved the world that he gave his one and only Son" (John 3:16).

The path to maturity begins with a study of the meaning of true love. One of my most treasured books is a first edition of W. E. Sangster's *The Path to Perfection*. In this little-known work, he writes

> "It is a calamity that the word 'love' is so wide, so blurred, so amorphous. We use the same term to cover the flutterings of adolescent emotion in spring, and the mighty passion which moves in the heart of God. Into this one [English] word we pour in sad and profane confusion [no less than five Greek words]."[1]

Sangster continues:

> "The English word 'love' invites us, yet obstructs us. . . . It is too shallow because it is too wide. . . . The plain man persists in using the word as though love were only an emotion. . . . But feelings fluctuate. If love were only present when the feeling-tone is strong enough to be self-conscious, every form of human affection would be a poor and intermittent thing. Feeling is affected

by health, circumstances, and physical comfort. . . . The restless tides of feeling can never be a true index to a deep and constant love. . . . True love is ingenious, strategic, resourceful, indestructible, seeking, serving, praying, bleeding. Here is love in feeling, thought, and will."[2]

Love in action.

In the letters of the apostle John, we read similar words: "Let us not love with words or tongue but with actions and in truth" (1 John 3:18). The power of John's message became most clear to me in my first parish through a young man named Bobby. Bobby had a profound learning disability. At age eighteen, he could barely read at a kindergarten level. When I started teaching a confirmation class—a training course to prepare children for full membership in the church—I discovered that Bobby had never been confirmed. We invited him to join the class. It was a tradition that on Confirmation Sunday each student would memorize a favorite verse of scripture and recite it before the congregation as he or she was received into membership. Bobby chose a passage from 1 John, just three words he could remember but three words that held more meaning than all the books of rhetoric and philosophy combined: "God is love."

The congregation knew Bobby as the embodiment of God's love, because despite his mental deficiencies, Bobby always had a smile, a hug, or a kind word for everyone. That Sunday morning, as he loudly and proudly pronounced his memory verse—"God is love!"—I felt like a spiritual midget compared to Bobby.

Years later, when I was watching the blockbuster movie *Forrest Gump*, I thought of Bobby as the similarly impaired Forrest told his dying girlfriend that he loved her. She said something to the effect that he didn't know what he was saying. Forrest replied, "I may be stupid, I may not know a lot of things. . .*but I know what love is!*" By then, of course, everyone in the theater had seen that Forrest Gump had a better grasp on true love than any other character in the movie.

I may be stupid, but I know what love is.

~~~

Notes

1. W. E. Sangster, *Path to Perfection* (Nashville: Abingdon-Cokesbury, 1943), 147.

2. Ibid., 150–53.

MISTAKE NUMBER TWO

"I'M TRYING TO FIX THE UNHAPPY PEOPLE AROUND ME"

Mistake Number Two
"I'm Trying to Fix the Unhappy People around Me"

Comedian Woody Allen is a world-class neurotic, even if his bleak pessimism is somewhat tongue-in-cheek. Here's a typical Woodyism: "We stand today at a crossroads: One path leads to despair and utter hopelessness. The other leads to total extinction. Let us hope we have the wisdom to make the right choice." He also once said, "There are two kinds of people in the world: the horrible. . .and the miserable." Neurotics like Allen may be surprised to learn that not everyone is horribly unhappy. And I have more news for you:

You don't have to fix unhappy people in order to be happy yourself!

Loving other people does not make us solely responsible for making them happy. Yes, Jesus challenges us to love others, even to lay down our lives for them if need be. But He did not say we should lie down and become emotional doormats. If letting other people walk all over me would be a good thing for their health and growth, I might consider it as part of my Christian duty. However, it is far more helpful for them, and for me, that I make them responsible for their own emotional maturity. The greater truth is that I cannot "fix" other people's unhappiness; they must choose for themselves their mental and spiritual state.

Can you accept this important principle in dealing with miserable and negative people? Admit it: You can love them, but you can't force them to love you back, and you can't force them to be happy. And God does not expect you to forfeit your happiness just because others prefer to be miserable. Indeed, the Golden Rule ("Do unto others. . .") and the Great Commandment ("Love God and love your neighbor") compel us to care about folks who have genuine pain in their lives. But we are not made more effective at caring about and reaching out to the unfortunate by our neurotic tendency to blame ourselves for the world's misfortunes. We are not obligated to do the impossible! This bears repeating: Many miserable people *choose* to be unhappy (either consciously or subconsciously). If we try to make them happy, we are violating their free will—and wasting our time. Consider the following illustration.

Susie Mae was frowning. She was sharing a coffee break with a coworker, Julia, and had already begun a familiar litany of the woes in her life. "I am so sick of my boss. . .he never listens to me, he constantly looks down on me, he never appreciates my work. . ."

Her list of complaints against him would have continued for several minutes, but sweet Julia interrupted,

"That's why I wanted to have coffee with you. I just heard that he's being promoted to another department. You are free of him, Susie Mae!"

Susie Mae replied, "I can't believe they are promoting that jerk!" She then launched into a tirade against the company as a whole, its unfair promotion policies, and her certain knowledge that she, Susie Mae the Discriminated Against, would never get such a promotion.

Julia tried to change the subject—"Hey, I heard that your husband sent you a big bouquet of roses last week"—but Susie Mae was unfazed.

"Oh yes, indeed. The jerk was trying to make up for the way he'd treated me. He went hunting with his buddies and left the screaming kids with me all day Saturday. He thought bringing home a deer would 'endear' him to me, and he used that as an excuse for why he was gone so long."

Again Julia tried to steer for calmer waters. "Well, just last month you were complaining about the price of beef. The free venison surely helped your grocery bill."

Susie Mae was up to the challenge. "Don't take that lazy bum's side!"

"Now, Susie Mae, your husband works a fifty-hour week at the plant; he loves you dearly; and from what I can see, he isn't gone as much as my golfing husband. And frankly, I'm kinda glad Joe is out of my hair sometimes. He comes back from the course a much happier man."

Not to be deterred, Susie Mae continued to whine

about how easy it was for Julia since she didn't have to deal with kids, and so on. Julia started to say that she and Joe would give anything to have two beautiful kids like Susie Mae's and how difficult the adoption process was proving to be, but Susie Mae continued to steer the conversation back to her own complaints. Finally the coffee break ended as it dawned on Julia that her attempts to cheer up her friend were like pearls to pigs. Susie Mae, for her part, went home to her loving husband, who patiently listened as she reported how totally unsympathetic her coworker had been and how "Julia's so smug and happy with her preppie husband, and she lords it over me."

It should be clear to us as detached observers that Susie Mae, in an unhealthy way, thoroughly enjoys being a whiner and resents Julia's well-intentioned efforts to fix things. Susie Mae savors the role of victim. Feeling sorry for herself, viewing the world as a harsh and unfair place, and reveling in her "bad luck" saves her from facing the fact that she has never taken responsibility for her own choices and failures. Misery is her friend. But Julia goes home with a burden of anxiety for Susie Mae. She feels guilty for enjoying her job and her husband. At day's end, as Julia lays her head on the pillow, she expends a great deal of emotional energy thinking of things she might do tomorrow to brighten up Susie Mae's life. Pity them both!

Everybody knows a Susie Mae. And Julia, while not as deeply troubled as Susie Mae, has her own burdens that stem from a misunderstanding about what love calls us to do. Sometimes love calls us to be tough-minded, when the most loving thing to do is to be direct and painfully honest with someone. God never intended for love to be disconnected from common sense. To the contrary, true love is inextricably bound to wisdom and truth. As 1 Corinthians 13:6 puts it, "Love does not delight in evil but rejoices with the truth." And we should not love adults the same way we love children. Adult love does not soft-peddle, coddle, or co-opt. Exercising mature love means we are to be "speaking the truth in love" (Ephesians 4:15) and challenging those around us also to strive for maturity. Jesus spoke of love as a challenge. He said, "If you love me, you will obey what I command" (John 14:15). Love is tied to proper action. The love to which God calls us is not sentimental mush; it is strong, active, and resolute—it is simultaneously about forgiveness and telling the truth. Love is not for sissies.

I occasionally bump into personalities even more toxic than Susie Mae's—people who not only see their world through dark, distorted glasses but who also view *me* dimly, with scathing, critical disdain. While I am a sinner, I am not a wicked person. Hopefully my readers can say the same. We work hard, we obey the law and pay our taxes, go to church, care about other people, love everyone the best we can, give to the poor, etc. Nevertheless, to the toxic criticizers, I am pond scum. As a neurotic, it took me thirty years to realize that *I* was not the problem—they were. Toxic criticizers never find anyone in their lives who measures up—with one possible exception: They are sometimes enamored with other toxic criticizers who join them in a mutual "hate-fest" as they jointly run down the rest of the world.

I once worked with a pleasant young lady, and we shared a cranky boss. Nothing I did ever seemed to be good enough. He constantly carried a scowl for me and ran me down behind my back. I lost a good deal of sleep feeling bad about myself and contemplating what I might have done to have offended the boss—and how to win him over. Self-absorbed in my own low self-esteem, it took me months to observe that almost invariably when a customer would exit our store, the boss would comment nastily, "I don't like him." Finally, when he remarked to me that he did not like my coworker, a lightbulb turned on in my head. She was such a pleasant and good person! If the boss thought ill of her, maybe it didn't matter that he thought ill of me. He clearly disliked *everyone*, yet I was foolish enough to believe that somehow I could win him over to my fan club.

That is an interesting paradox about us neurotics. We have low self-esteem, yet we hold delusions of grandeur that somehow we can fix the world and cure the toxic criticizers of their disease. In hindsight, there was no way I could have made that wicked boss fond of me—he didn't even like himself! The only way I could have changed his lifelong habit of hating the world would have been to toss a toaster in his hot tub. If you are laughing, my reader friend, it is probably because this hyperbolic humor uncovers your own anger at such people and the deep pain they have caused. A secret part of you would like to kill them! Which brings us to a bigger point: the need to call evil *evil*.

The Bible devotes many of its chapters to the topic of evil people and their wicked deeds. In contrast, its pages never give a textbook definition of evil. You will not find a detailed epistemology of Satan in scripture. But the Bible clearly warns us that we are in the middle of a cosmic battle between active forces of good and evil.

Our postmodern age scoffs at the notion of a devil and is reticent to label anything or anyone as truly evil. Hitler's Holocaust and the 9/11 terrorist attacks have shaken that view; reasonable people agree these were truly evil events. Yet somehow, in our gentle "lambs and bunnies" Sunday school mind-set, we are still slow to name a particular individual as evil.

Perhaps because Jesus told us not to judge, we feel disallowed the luxury of calling someone evil. But Jesus also said, "Why don't you judge for yourselves what is right?" (Luke 12:57). Without going into a long contextual study of what Jesus really meant by saying, "Do not judge, or you too will be judged" (Matthew 7:1), let me suggest that *discerning reality* is not the same as openly judging, sentencing, and punishing a person. As Christians, we are indeed called to distinguish right from wrong and good from evil. Jesus did not hesitate to call certain people evil—the Pharisees in particular—and He explained that "by their fruit you will recognize them" (Matthew 7:20). The Bible encourages us to be discerning. In 1 Corinthians 5, Paul gives the church permission to judge and deal harshly with wicked people. Hebrews 5:14 instructs us to "distinguish good from evil." Scripture warns us against being naive: " 'Be as shrewd as snakes and as innocent as doves' " (Matthew 10:16). Paul told the church in Rome, "Love must be sincere. Hate what is evil; cling to what is good" (Romans 12:9).

Open your eyes to the reality that some people around you are toxically evil. If you can't bring yourself to call them *evil*, call them "N-types." Some people—thankfully a tiny, rare number—are *No* people, filled with *no*s and *no*gativity. N-types are *no*gligent, *no*xious, *no*sey, *no*rcissistic, *no*sty, *no*y-saying *no*-it-alls. They are borderline psychotics, rarely aware of their own evil. N-types do not care who they hurt. They are so concerned with getting their *own* way they will crush those *in* their way. They feed on unhappiness, both their own and others'.

N-types are not criminals in the usual sense of the word. They obey the law to the letter, and they will rarely see the inside of a jail cell. But they can be identified by the turmoil and anxiety in their wake. The N-type will throw the grown-up version of a temper tantrum just often enough to keep everyone in their circle of intimates on edge. The N-type knows instinctively that most people like to avoid conflict, so he or she holds the peace hostage in order to rule. Here's an example—I'll call her Yvonne.

Yvonne had money. Never mind that she did not earn the money—she was nonetheless proud of her wealth and used it as leverage on anyone who needed her money, whether they were friends, employees in her family firm, or the family itself. Yvonne's limited power combined with some serious personality flaws to give her both the confidence and the motive to run down other people in their absence. If the persons in question confronted Yvonne, she would lie to cover up her sin. In the rare event that someone called her hand with the truth, Yvonne would attack her accuser viciously. So timid folks would usually shrink from her. This only emboldened Yvonne to exert more power.

I have had some success standing up to bullying N-types like Yvonne. It requires a balancing act of firm personal strength with a patient love that can see through the N-type's tough facade. But more often than not, I find N-types have so embraced the persona of selfishness and lies that they cannot be helped. . .nor do they even *want* to be helped.

Unfortunately, as neurotics in search of love, we devote a great deal of wasted energy trying in vain to fix these people. The N-types sense this and respond by making our lives miserable. Psychotic N-types love only one thing: eating neurotics for breakfast.

In this chapter, I am being purposely graphic and forthright in describing the problem. I'm guessing you need to hear it. You are seeking God and love without recognizing that evil doesn't want you to find either. So here's an even more explicit illustration.

I recently read a gripping account of an animal-loving nature photographer who moved into the Alaskan wilderness to film and study grizzly bears. He was a dedicated pacifist who believed that patience, caring, kindness, and empathy could soothe the savage beast. His goal was to convince others that these dangerous carnivores have been unfairly maligned. He camped for months at a time in the midst of grizzly country without a weapon, demonstrating that by mimicking the bears' movements and sounds (he claimed to have learned their language) he could mingle with the huge animals safely. Once, he even gained the trust of a mother and her cubs— usually thought of as the riskiest of encounters because of the bears' instinctive, motherly defensiveness—and he lay down among them without harm. He even persuaded a girlfriend to join him in his efforts to befriend and protect these creatures, ignoring the fact that grizzly bears weigh over half a ton and can tear the head off a moose with one swipe of their claws. Bears routinely dig their sharp fangs into the flesh of their prey, not necessarily out of evil but simply as part of their survival instinct. Whatever the motive, one night a hungry grizzly invaded their camp. The photographer, video camera running, left the tent to gently confront the bear, confident that his singsong cooing could send the bear away. The videotape recorded the sounds of his encounter, but his songs quickly turned to screams of pain and cries of "It's not working!" and "I'm getting killed out here!" The naturalist's female companion tried more aggressively to fend off the vicious grizzly, but it was too little too late. Both were grotesquely eaten alive by the very creature they were trying to help, literally victims of their own nearsighted naïveté.

Let that graphic but true story help you break out of your naive notions about N-types. Be discerning. Some of the "grumpy bears" in your life are truly good people who just yearn for some TLC and attention. Under some crusty exteriors are needy people who will respond and soften when you touch them with genuine love. But some people do not want your help. Some will bite the hand that feeds them. If you try to hug *everybody*, just remember: Not all bear hugs are safe, and some things that appear warm and fuzzy can still kill you.

Turn to the next chapter to learn some methods for dealing with the toxic waste in your life—how to distinguish between the needy and the nasty, between the teddy bears and the grizzlies.

SOLUTION NUMBER TWO

"I WON'T BE A SLAVE TO THE JERKS IN MY LIFE"

Solution Number Two
"I Won't Be a Slave to the Jerks in My Life"

Let us assume that, having read this far, you are a highly sensitive person. You have been a prisoner of your own neurotic worries and carry a load of anxiety. It would be easy to blame the negative grizzlies in your life, but the truth is that your slavery to them and your prison of neuroses are self-imposed. Now is the time for you to announce your emancipation. Get in your car with the windows rolled up and yell, "I will no longer live down to the lowest common denominator of the jerks around me!" There is no virtue in allowing miserable people to make us miserable. Realizing that is the first step to emotional freedom.

The second step is to understand the dynamics of power. In the civilized, democratic world, no one has dictatorial power over your life unless you have given it to them. Hear it again: No one has power over your life unless you give them power. An example: Jason worked in a retail store with Blane, a tyrannical N-type boss. Blane constantly berated Jason, both as a person and as an employee. Even when Jason did well, which was often, the boss focused on some minor imperfection in Jason's performance. What Jason could not see was that he was

actually smarter than Blane. And Blane had his own set
of insecurities, but these were masked because, as the top
manager, he could squelch any dissent or criticism. Jason
lived in fear of the boss and spent many nights tossing and
turning, formulating elaborate plans as to how he might
win the boss's approval. Sadly, despite Jason's intelligence,
he overlooked the most obvious solution: The best way to
escape the tyranny was to leave the company! The mall
where he worked was filled with stores advertising for
more help. It would have been a simple matter to change
jobs. Instead, Jason lived in such neurotic fear that he
subconsciously linked his boss with his paycheck and thus
felt that his very existence depended upon Blane. So Jason
stayed put when all he needed to do was ask the employees
at some nearby stores whether they liked and respected
their bosses, and change employment accordingly.

I have a friend who recently was in a similar
situation. Not until his unpleasant job and N-type boss
drove him to the edge of a nervous breakdown did he find
the motivation (in this case, *pain*) to change jobs. He lived
in a small town and the new job paid a lower salary, but it
provided him with confidence and a better attitude, which
in turn enabled him to continue looking for a job that
better fit his abilities. A few months later, he found his
dream job and is now happier than ever.

Am I suggesting that the solution to all your on-
the-job worries is simply to quit or change jobs? No.
The bigger point is about perspective. The realization
that you are not an indentured servant, that you have

occupational options, should empower you to move away from fear to a place of confidence. The fact that you are reading this book means you are probably more motivated and intelligent than many of the people around you, and you are likely more valuable to your firm than you realize. Wake up and claim your competence! Then use your newfound confidence to rise above the negativity surrounding you. Perhaps only a few small irritations in your workplace are making you miserable. Going to your supervisor with confidence for a professional, heart-to-heart talk might easily resolve the situation without your having to change jobs. A rehearsed statement like this can work wonders: "Boss, I truly like working here and want to be the best employee I can be, but a couple of relatively minor problems are making my work far more stressful than it should be. Would you help me change my situation?" Only a truly evil boss would say, "No, I won't help you" (in which case, you *should* quit!). Most supervisors will ask what the problem is. In your response, be sure to offer a possible solution, not just a complaint. Your solution might even include a direct request for your boss to change his or her actions. For example, "You probably don't realize how it really upsets me when you do X or say Y. I was hoping you could instead do Z. If you can do that for me, I'll be a happier and more productive employee." Nine times out of ten, your life will get better once you recognize your competence, claim your independence, and gently assert yourself using direct, solutions-oriented requests.

Some of the same principles apply in non-occupational settings. Do some of your good friends—though they're generally friendly—have some inconsiderate or grating ways of occasionally speaking down to you? Let them know! True friendships will survive—and grow—when you stand up for yourself.

For some of us with full-blown neuroses, this is all easier said than done. We live in paralyzing fear of grizzly bear N-types. Understanding exactly how certain N-types create fear in us and manipulate our neuroses may require some deeper thought. Here are a few more morsels to consider:

- N-types are usually not smarter than you, but they *are* skilled (from years of practice) in their craft of criticizing and browbeating others. Therefore, you will have to focus intensely on strategies for outwitting them. Unfortunately, as a good and sensitive person, you have been expending your energy trying to please them or make them happy. Wrong focus. Use your energy to outsmart them, not to appease them.

- N-types know that in any group there are enough fearful neurotics that even if they lose power over one (like *you!*), they can still manipulate the others and thus control everyone. Most people fear and avoid conflict or confrontation and will bow to the whims of an N-type boss or coworker in order to keep the peace. But you might discover in a private, one-on-one setting, that everyone else has the same fear and low opinion of the N-type person—and if others only knew they were not alone in confronting the problem, they would show more courage. I have been amazed at how some of the biggest villains have been defeated when a second brave voice simply joined with mine in calling them to accountability. Here's my simplest advice: Buy your fellow oppressed neurotics a copy of this book!

• N-types are usually deeply insecure, but as with the example of Jason's boss, Blane, they have learned how to mask their insecurity. One of their tactics is to attack other people and put them on the defensive so that they don't have time to see the N-type's flaws. This might sound un-Christian, but sometimes it is liberating to make a list of an N-type's inadequacies. You don't need to share that list with anyone, but it will empower you simply to have it.

• For all their dominating skills and bluster, N-types are generally not very strong people. They are like hot-air balloons, easily pricked and deflated. However, a caution is in order: If you publicly deflate these evil balloons, they can lash out in irrational and destructive ways—just as when you let loose a real balloon and it flies erratically all around the room. You don't want to be caught out in the open if they explosively lash out. Rather than completely popping their balloon and destroying their overblown egos, it is far safer (and more effective) to subtly demonstrate that you have the knowledge and ability to take them on without actually doing it. Someone once told me, "If you plan to totally discredit, embarrass, or deflate a pompous ego in public, you should also plan to *kill* him, because otherwise he will try to kill you in mindless revenge." The best advice is Teddy Roosevelt's famous maxim: "Walk softly, and carry a big stick."

Far too many self-help books, many of them filled with clichés and oversimplifications, have been written about the importance of self-esteem. So I am hesitant to retrace old terrain. Still, a feeling of inferiority plagues many neurotics, sometimes because of a physical shortcoming that makes it very difficult for them to simply adopt the advice

I have given. If it will help to empower you, here are some thoughts about how to deal with a poor self-image:

An unattractive—or just plain ugly—face is an easy target for cruel jokes. Now, I'm no Brad Pitt. I was so ugly as a child, my mother had to tie a pork chop around my neck just to get the dog to play with me. No, I'm kidding. But old jokes like that about homely people have a way of sticking with a person. We sometimes believe and internalize comments meant strictly in jest. So we have to be careful with those kinds of cruel comments.

When I was in gymnastics class in college, a girl came out of the locker room one day and told our coach: "Gosh, who is that ugly woman I saw in the bathroom? Her face was all messed up. She has to be the ugliest woman I've seen in my life." The coach looked at her angrily and replied, "That's my wife." The girl nearly died of embarrassment. Lucky for her, the coach was only joking. He didn't know the lady, but you can bet that girl learned a memorable lesson. Remarks about people's looks can be cruel and painful. The face we see in the mirror, the face we present to the world, is very important for our sense of well-being.

Let me share a very personal account related to me by a seminary buddy of mine who has a disfigured face. Let's call him Joe. Listen to these words he wrote about himself:

I was born with a severe facial disfigurement and cleft palate. I would have died were it not for eleven operations I had as a child. My disfigurement caused me a lot of problems academically, but the major problems were social. I remember one incident from my fourth grade teacher. As a friend and I were playing together, the teacher said to my friend, "Don't play with him. . .he'll never amount to anything." I felt she was referring to my physical appearance.

In high school, being a teenager and not fitting the Hollywood image that women seemed to expect of men, I wasn't popular. When I left school, I joined the army, but even there the sergeant said, "You need to get that lip fixed or you'll never get promoted." I have felt rejected all my life. The real fact is that physical appearance totally determines one's success in life. I have a very real problem that has kept me single, prevented a good social life, and hurt me in school. I have been called by God but feel I have no gifts or abilities.

Joe's despair touched my heart. When he read those words aloud in our therapy group, I found it hard to answer. In some ways, he is right: Our society puts too much emphasis on skin-deep appearance. We act like beauty is the mark of goodness; we make idols out of Hollywood stars; we envy the "beautiful people."

But as Joe and I went through seminary together, we both grew up a lot. We began to learn that God's plan has nothing to do with how we look outwardly and everything to do with who we are inwardly. Though God created a beautiful world, he chose to come to earth in a very plain fashion. In the book of Isaiah, we have a messianic prophecy that may be the only physical description of Jesus: "He had no beauty or majesty to attract us to him, nothing in his appearance that we should desire him. . .and we esteemed him not" (Isaiah 53:2–3).

Jesus was not one of "the beautiful people." There was nothing beautiful about the cross, either. It was a dirty, bloody, stinking mess of a way for God to present Himself to the world as Savior. But we prefer not to think of God that way. We are like Joe—we accept the myth that only beautiful things can be good.

Certainly Joe had problems beyond his control. But his biggest problem was that he had believed society's lie—the lie that beauty is the mark of success. A companion lie is that if society labels us as an ugly failure, we must be one.

God uses a different valuation and a different plan. The first inch of human skin counts for very little in God's assessment—after all, by God's design our skin-deep beauty fades as we age. And God has a power that transcends cosmetics. In Colossians, Paul announced that Christians have "put off [the] old self. . .and. . .put on the new" (Ephesians 4:22, 24). This is more than the donning of fancy clothes or new makeup. It is a complete transformation of our inner being, totally independent of what society does or thinks. Paul also said, "Clothe yourselves with compassion, kindness, humility, gentleness and patience" (Colossians 3:12). That new clothing is a spiritual garment. And it has a way of shining through the roughest exterior.

Let me tell you of another friend with a physical deformity. Tommy was born with a birth defect that caused giantism in his hands. They looked grossly swollen, about three sizes bigger than they should have been in proportion to his body. They were not pretty to look at; they made him look like a comic book character, a real-life caricature. Yet Tommy never let his birth defect stop him. He received a college education, became a successful architect, and married a beautiful woman. He gave himself to Christ and devoted himself to work in the church. And here's the amazing thing: When Tommy took those big, fat, ugly hands and placed them on a piano, out would pour the most splendid music you've ever heard. Once you came to know Tommy, you would never view him as abnormal or blemished. The grace of his spirit, like the beauty of his music, overshadowed his physical deformity.

Because of his disease, Tommy died as a young man. He has now been given a new and glorified body, perfect in the image of God. But even before his heavenly transformation, Christ living in Tommy made him a beautiful human being.

My old friend with the cleft palate, Joe, is beginning to learn what Tommy knew: that beauty is an inward thing. Joe does not have to wait until that heavenly day when he shall have a different face. Christianity offers it to us today—if only we could see it. Paul wrote in 1 Corinthians 13:12, "Now we see in a mirror, dimly, but then we will see face to face" (NRSV). In heaven we will see our true face, our real self, our actual appearance, uncluttered by the artificialities and pretenses of this life. In heaven we will bear the likeness of Christ. And we can begin— starting today!—to become Christlike through a beauty of heart and action.

For now, we must see by faith that God is giving us new selves, new faces. Too often we let the opinions of the world mold us. We let our self-esteem, our self-worth, be set by the world's opinion of our outer appearance. But if we allow the world to determine our inner beauty, we can all too easily be molded into a monstrous apparition.

C. S. Lewis wrote a marvelous book about beauty titled *Till We Have Faces*. Let me summarize his story:

Once upon a time, a princess was born with a plain and homely face. Her sisters were beautiful, but all she felt was rejection for her ugliness. The princess blamed all her problems on her external unattractiveness. She began to wear a veil to hide her face and retreated from meaningful human companionship. She grew envious of her sisters and distrustful of everyone else. Upon inheriting the throne, she became a petty, mean, and cynical ruler, taking out her bitterness on all those around her.

Toward the end of her life, a messenger from God told the princess the truth: "*You were never ugly*. True, you weren't as beautiful as your sisters. You were plain and nothing special, but never *ugly*. And your sisters envied you. . .you were smarter than they were, more capable, brave, and destined to inherit the throne."

The messenger continued to enlighten the princess: "You were not ugly, but you allowed yourself to nurse self-pity, to dwell on your physical limitations rather than on your gifts. You became bitter in heart, as ugly and faceless on the inside as you had imagined yourself to be outwardly."

Through that book, C. S. Lewis was giving us this message: We are all born without faces—blank slates ready to be written upon. We must not sit idly by waiting for someone to magically bestow beauty or talent or strength or smarts upon us. We must realize that both our inner and outer beauty are mostly a function of what we *decide* to become—or, more correctly, what we allow God to create in us.

As a PK (preacher's kid) and a pastor myself, I have moved around more than most people in life and have found this to be true: The people who strike me as absolutely handsome when I first meet them sometimes turn out to be dull and empty and not so attractive in the long run. And others, whose faces upon first impression seem plain, or even goofy-looking, later change as I come to know them. Over time, their inner spiritual beauty comes shining through. It is almost as if they develop a new face. Then I no longer remember them as they appeared at our first superficial encounter. Have you ever experienced this?

Thankfully God not only sees us as we are, but as what we are *going* to be once we receive our new faces. Listen again to the apostle Paul, this time in Romans

8:18–19: "I consider that our present sufferings are not worth comparing with the glory that will be revealed in us. The creation waits in eager expectation for the sons of God to be revealed." You see, God has planned from the start of creation to reveal in you a glorious being, a son or daughter of God! Paul continues his argument in Romans 12:2: "Do not conform any longer to the pattern of this world, but be transformed." Or as the Phillips translation puts it, "Don't let the world around you squeeze you into its own mould, but let God re-mould your minds from within." God wants to give you a new face—one of confidence that reveals your inner beauty and virtue.

The empowerment, grace, and permission you've received to free you from low self-esteem and neurotic bondage to the unhappiness of others comes with a warning label: Christians are called to care for and love our neighbors. The Christian journey is a narrow path, a tightrope. On one side, filled with low self-esteem, you can fall into neurotic, codependent behavior, where the N-types rob you of abundant living. On the other side is the abyss of callous selfishness and arrogance. Successful, mature Christian living requires us to watch our steps. Some N-types are very needy people, and our approach to them should be one of tough love, but love and caring nonetheless.

The truth is, most of the N-types I've known have been blessed with material prosperity and a supportive family, and any attempt to show them kindness will be met with contempt. Moreover, their grasping, self-centered, whining narcissism can draw our eyes away from the truly needy. The poor and the spiritually lost have a much greater need for our love and care—and our outreach to them can truly make a difference. This is why Jesus said the poor and the meek are blessed—they are receptive to love. N-types can only be helped when *they* decide to change.

As Christians, we are called to have concern and love for others. First John tells us clearly that the best way to give love to *God* is to first love our *neighbor*. But we need to think carefully about the specific ways we can do that. John does not mince words. He states boldly, "If anyone says, 'I love God,' yet hates his brother, he is a liar" (1 John 4:20).

We have choices to make in the use of love. The Greek word for Christian love is *agapé*. Agapé refers not to feelings but to an intentional, targeted love. It is a love that is not rooted in the emotions but in the mind. We can choose to love people even if we don't particularly like them. It is refreshing and empowering to begin being nice to people not out of fear, self-protection, or neurotic compulsion, but out of a choice to love them despite their flaws.

Finding freedom from our unpleasant relationships and thoughts regarding the jerks and N-types in our lives does not happen by reading one chapter in a self-help book. In the following chapters, particularly the next two, you will find more ideas and tactics for making life bearable in the presence of perturbing people. A sense of humor helps. Laughing over your enemies' quirks is a lot better than killing them!

MISTAKE NUMBER THREE

"I CAN'T STOP RELIVING THE PAST"

Mistake Number Three
"I Can't Stop Reliving the Past"

Highly sensitive people spend much of their time living inside their heads, dwelling in their thoughts rather than in the outer world. That's not all bad. The world of inner thought is as vital as the material world. According to Socrates and other famous ancient philosophers, being thoughtful and contemplative beats the unexamined life. At issue is the *quality* of our thoughts. Our time in this life is finite. Every minute we spend living in the past, dwelling mentally on the problems of yesterday, is a minute we cannot spend on enjoying the present or building our future!

For some of us neurotic types, we almost can't help ourselves. It is like an old, never-ending eight-track tape that has the tape wound in a circle; when all the songs have been played, it starts again with the first song. We replay the excruciating embarrassments of yesterday, the mistakes of last week, the ugly arguments of a month ago. As the mental tape plays again and again, we not only lose the time it takes to relive those events, but we also feel the wretched emotions again, as if the negative moment were still with us. We have trouble understanding that the past has indeed *passed*.

Years ago, an acquaintance treated me unfairly and rudely. I was angry. Still, the slight against me had no lasting significance. With nothing to gain by pursuing the matter, the best thing I could have done was to let it go. Instead, I kept replaying the scene in my head. How dare that guy act so curtly! How right I was and how wrong he was! The next day was a beautiful blue-sky day, and I was out on the water with my family, riding a slalom ski over the waves—but rather than enjoy my favorite sport, I was in mental agony as the eight-track tape in my head kept replaying my bitterness. Even in the midst of the adrenaline thrill of jumping the boat's wake, misery gripped my mind. My subconscious mind kept repeating the incident with the misplaced hope that somehow the scene would reach a different ending and I could find justice. What a foolish illusion! Finding justice in the present is tough enough; seeking fairness in what happened yesterday is almost always an exercise in futility.

I suppose there is a time for righteous anger. On a few occasions in my life, people have truly done me wrong or intentionally wanted to hurt me. But even then, stewing over the injustice, steeping ourselves in bitterness, hurts us far more than it does those who wronged us. We must find a way to stop reliving the pain, or else our simmering anger will eat us up inside.

Does anger ever really feel good? Well, it feels good to *vent* our anger, I suppose, but only because anger is such an unpleasant thing to harbor in the first place.

Venting our anger in nondestructive ways is healthy. But holding on to our bitterness is like the foolishness depicted in a Gary Larson *Far Side* cartoon. The picture shows a family of rats gathered around the kitchen table while Mama Rat is opening the cupboard for breakfast. There, amid the cereal boxes, is a box labeled "Rat Poison." In the caption, Mama Rat says, "You know, we probably shouldn't keep the rat poison next to the cereal. . . . In fact, why do we even *have* this stuff?" Bitterness is a poison that has no place in our cupboards!

Rage and resentment are often the cause of stress-related diseases. Constantly angry people are unhealthy people. They can't enjoy life. They can't enjoy relationships. It saddens me when I see families that can't enjoy togetherness because they are so quick to take offense and so slow to forgive. Healthy relationships can endure honest expressions of frustration and irritation, but no relationship will be helped by constant expressions of animosity.

Forgiveness is the cure for resentment. And as it frees us from replaying our grudges, forgiveness can be a tremendously redemptive and healing force in the lives of those around us.

For years after a twelve-year-old boy in California witnessed the murder of his father, he was bitter, apathetic, and withdrawn. Psychologists were of no help. As the boy grew older, his anger gnawed at him so much that he could not give his heart to anything or anyone. But as an adult, he found Christ, and over time, he began to work through his bitterness, to brighten up and enjoy life. He realized that life was too short for hatred. Through the grace of God, he was able to do an amazing thing. He forgave his father's murderer and even visited him in prison.

The first visit was awkward and unpleasant for both parties. But the Christian man did not give up. He returned again and again and told the prisoner, "God wiped my slate clean of my sins. I'm willing to do the same for you, to forgive and acquit you of the terrible crime you committed against me by killing my father." He then went on to prove it. When the prisoner was later paroled, this man helped him get a job and start a new life. Eventually the prisoner's heart softened, and he, too, accepted Christ. The spirit of forgiveness had healed them both.

You may say, "I have tried, but I can't find it in my heart to forgive that person who hurt me so deeply and wronged me so wickedly!" Well, if nothing else, try pity! What I mean is this: Try to find a deeper understanding of the psychology behind your enemy. Generally people who are mean and irritable have some underlying burden or problem in their personality or background that makes them so irascible. It is hard to hate someone for whom you feel pity!

One of the few people I have ever hated was a boat motor mechanic. I had purchased a used outboard motor from this fellow—we'll call him Damon—based on his promise that it ran great and that he would back it up with a warranty. He also took my old motor on consignment. When it turned out that the motor Damon had sold me did not run well, I returned it for repair. It sat untouched in his shop all summer, and as I watched other people enjoying the lake with their boats, my anger toward Damon grew and grew. The salt in my wound came when I discovered that he had sold my trade-in and pocketed the money. So he had lied to me, stolen my money—twice— and left me with nothing but his curt, cranky tone. I was seething. Only when I threatened him with a lawsuit did Damon finally offer to make things right. He asked me to come to his shop to settle up with him. The shop was noisy and busy and filled with many other disgruntled customers ahead of me, so I sat and waited. While I waited, I watched as Damon dealt with one angry customer after another—people who were justifiably angry with him because he had also mistreated them. I gradually began to get a picture of his unenviable life. After a while, his little boy came in and asked for something, and Damon snapped at him. A bit later, his wife came in, and he yelled at her, too. I looked in her eyes and saw that any love she once might have had for her husband was now gone. I began to put together this picture: Damon's life was soon going to be in shambles, his wife would leave him, his son would grow up embittered, and his business would suffer—all because he could not control his anger. In that moment, I no longer hated Damon; I pitied him. That may not be the best way to deal with hatred toward an enemy, but it worked for me.

The problem of living in the past is bigger than just remembering our problematic and painful episodes.

Sometimes people reminisce about a romanticized "golden age" or "the good ol' days" and fail to be present for the joys of today. In hindsight, the past often looks better than it really was. Our selective memories may overstate the goodness of yesterday and prevent us from moving forward into a better tomorrow.

Jesus said that anyone who puts his hand to the plow and looks back is not ready for the kingdom of God (Luke 9:62). He was teaching us that leaning into the future is the posture needed for kingdom living. This forward-leaning posture is easier described than adopted. For neurotics, the future is filled with peril—dark and unknown. The future brings fear more than promise. But this is not a biblical view. The very definition of faith includes the promise of eternal life, and even in this life at least a 50/50 chance that tomorrow will be better than today. God promises life abundant and life eternal. Have faith!

This book is a guide to God, so I ask you to think beyond your own personal psychology. I hope you yearn to enrich your knowledge of God out of a pure desire for a deeper relationship with your Creator. But a secondary benefit is that the more we learn about God and the more we rely upon faith, the better picture we get of our full human potential.

We are all familiar with the famous saying by George Santayana, "Those who fail to learn from history are doomed to repeat it." Certainly our past has great value; only a fool would ignore the lessons that can be gleaned by evaluating past failures (and successes). But learning from the past and being a passive victim of the past are two different things. God is a God of history. The Bible does not teach us to abandon the past or blot it from our memories. The Jewish festivals were aimed at reliving and celebrating their national history. Jesus even said, "Do this in remembrance of me" (Luke 22:19). But history is only a tiny part of the Bible's "recommended curriculum" for life. Much of the Bible is about living in the present and preparing for the future. The Old Testament prophets were always looking forward. Jesus spoke often about the coming kingdom of God as our joyful future. God is a God of history; yet even more so He's a God of future-living. For every moment that Jesus complained about the woeful state of His enemies, the Pharisees, He added twice as much time speaking parables about the future, about the way things ought to be in the coming kingdom of God.

Now if those forward-looking parables were only pipe dreams, they would be just as much a waste of time as reliving the dead past. But that is not the case. Jesus taught us about the future because the future will one day be the present—God's promises for us *will come true!* In a sense, any mental exertion that does not help us prepare for the future is wasted time. As Jesus says in Matthew 6:20, "Store up for yourselves treasures in heaven, where moth and rust do not destroy." This leads us into the next chapter as we consider some positive, practical ways by which we can learn from the past, live in the present, and prepare for the future.

SOLUTION NUMBER THREE

"LEARN FROM YESTERDAY,
PLAN FOR TOMORROW,
LIVE TODAY"

Solution Number Three
"Learn from Yesterday, Plan for Tomorrow, Live Today"

The difference between worrying and planning is like the difference between a penguin flapping its wings and an eagle soaring. The mechanics are very similar, but the results are oceans apart. The same energy you apply to worrying about yesterday and dreading tomorrow could be applied to planning and preparing for a better life in the future. And you can begin living that life today.

The smartest neurotic can be dumb with worry. We find it difficult to redirect our anxious energies because we've built up a lifetime of experience in habitual worry. This chapter offers some tips on how to transform fretting into forward-thinking productivity. The first step is to define *worry* and distinguish it from *contemplative planning*.

Worry is usually focused on one or more of the following: yesterday; a negative possibility for tomorrow; or a problem that is unsolvable. Worry replays the past, which can't be changed, or grinds away on tomorrow's irrelevant "crises." What makes a crisis *irrelevant*? When it can't be prevented, can't be solved, or simply won't ever happen. Worrywarts need to break the cycle by asking a direct question: "Can I honestly do much about that?" If the answer is, "Probably not," then it is time to change the subject.

By "changing the subject," I mean finding something—*anything*—to engage the mind and heart. If nothing productive or useful can be found, sometimes it is okay to resort to cheap, escapist entertainment: a pulp fiction book or a sitcom. When television producer Norman Lear was diagnosed with cancer, he wasted countless hours worrying about his illness and many more days feeling sorry for himself before he finally concluded that he needed to get his mind off of his troubles and put some joy into his life. He rented videotapes of classic comedy movies, such as the Marx Brothers and Laurel and Hardy, and watched them constantly until laughter crowded out his feelings of worry and sickness. He credits laughter for his recovery from cancer.

Maybe for you it will be enough to simply admit that replaying yesterday's problems is counterproductive. Armed with that clear knowledge, you may be able to make a firm decision to stop those destructive thoughts in their tracks and think of better things. If you have difficulty turning off your never-ending negativity tape, you may have deeper psychological issues that will require action beyond merely reading this book.

For me, years of group therapy and counseling did not seem to help much, particularly with my dark feelings of anxiety, dread, and depression. Finally a psychologist suggested I try antidepressant medication, specifically a new (at the time) product designed to block the brain's "serotonin uptake." It's a clever solution for those of us who do not have adequate levels of the neurotransmitter serotonin in the areas of the brain that affect mood and emotion. Instead of adding a dangerous imitation of serotonin to the body, these antidepressants merely slow the body's uptake and reabsorption of naturally occurring serotonin, resulting in more efficient use of this important electrochemical fluid that connects the nerve cells in our brain. In most cases, the effect is gradual and subtle, so the drug is not addictive, nor does it produce euphoria or marked side effects. Instead, it has freed me from constant anxiety and made a huge improvement in my ability to handle stress. I now feel the way "normal" people have always felt! Of course, different people react differently to the various versions of these antidepressants, but in my case, I have learned that a small daily dose is more effective (and has fewer side effects) than a large dose.

Many people who suffer from depression, anxiety, or social phobias have been hesitant to take my advice to see a psychiatrist in order to seek a prescription for antidepressant medication. They are more comfortable going to their family doctor, who can also write the needed prescription. For some, the stigma of a being "mentally ill" or visiting a "shrink" has kept them from taking action beyond visiting their pastor. I remind them that, in many cases, we are not talking about a spiritual issue or a moral failure but simply a chemical deficiency in the brain. If you were a diabetic and had insufficient levels of insulin, would you take medicine to treat that? Of course you would. Clinical depression is no different. You may well have a physiological deficiency and need medicine to correct it.

This does not mean we should abandon the traditional methods of "talk therapy" offered by psychologists, psychiatrists, and Christian counselors. Neuroses, depression, social anxiety, and obsessive-compulsive disorders are often triggered by stressful events in our world or are exacerbated by emotional baggage from our childhood. There is power in bringing an objective professional into your confidence to help you "unpack your emotional baggage" and to work with you in seeking pragmatic solutions to life's problems. Therapy may help you sort out unresolved issues of the past, so consider the big difference between passively replaying mental tape and actively working through a past trauma.

Another practical tip for fighting neurosis is to keep a list (either set aside in your memory or actually written on a note card) of "positive replacement thoughts" ready to "plug in" when needed. Or if you can't seem to control your thoughts, you may find it easier to control your actions. One way to change your inner world is to change your outer world. Delve into an unrelated work problem. If you are retired or have time on your hands, cultivate a hobby. When negative thoughts assail you, jump into gardening, paint-by-numbers, piano, or whatever excites you. When I'm stressed out, I strap on my electric guitar and turn the volume up loud. It works wonders!

Social anxiety is often a function of an insecure ego—which *all* humans have! When circumstances or conflicts in relationships arise that threaten a person's comfort zone, anxiety levels begin to rise. Stress causes physiological and psychological changes: a reversion to the "reptilian" brain, the primal survival instinct; a tightening of blood flow; less rational thinking; and an inability to hear another person's position. If you are an anxious person by nature, you must recognize that you are part of the problem. It is counterproductive to put your energy into trying to convince anxious persons not to be anxious. To lead them to a new viewpoint, the first priority is to lower their anxiety level by listening calmly to their fears rather than dwelling on your own nervous state. Remaining calm in an anxious situation may alleviate the strain far better than shifting into a high state of energy and fretting over how to "fix" things. In situations of conflict, stress, or abrasive tension, the first order of business is to calm yourself, and the second step is to slowly and smoothly bring calm to others. Humor can work wonders to diffuse highly volatile emotional moments, but it must be used carefully and selectively. Hear it again: The first priority in times of stress is to get outside your own angst and focus on becoming calm. It has an almost magical effect on group dynamics. In short, the only sure way to reduce the collective anxiety of a group is to find tranquillity yourself.

Of course, there is also a place for using your intelligence for problem solving and advance planning to lower your blood pressure. The terrain of worry and the landscape of constructive planning appear identical, but they lie on opposite sides of a grand canyon. As stated in the previous chapter, planning and building for tomorrow are the opposite of wasting time reliving the past. Planning is an investment; but worry only depletes your emotional bank account.

Even better than mental planning is physical preparation. For example, if you are worrying about your finances, get out your credit card bills and start making phone calls to reduce your interest rates. Or if your financial situation is dire and your nervous-energy level is high, find an enjoyable second job for a short time until you pay down your debt. If your stress level is mainly due to an unpleasant coworker, get one of the many available self-help books and learn how to deal with difficult people. If the coworker, or your boss, is a true monster, focus your energy into combing the want ads or updating your résumé. Taking action always beats wallowing in worry.

The happiest people are those who follow the Latin credo *Carpe diem*. "Seize the day!" As they say when it comes to comedy, timing is everything. In almost all things, if you take action too quickly *or* too slowly, you will fail. This is demonstrated by several contradictory—but equally true—aphorisms: "He who hesitates is lost," yet "Haste makes waste." "Strike while the iron is hot," yet "Fools rush in where angels fear to tread." Are you able to recognize when the time is right?

At the beginning of his ministry, Jesus announced that the time was fulfilled, the time was right (Mark 1:15). Without giving them much notice, Jesus called the disciples, and immediately they left their nets and followed Him. Jesus said to them, "The time is fulfilled," and they took Him literally. They grabbed the moment. They took action. The Gospels emphasize that they did not hesitate but followed Jesus immediately (Matthew 4:20, 22; Mark 1:18, 20; Luke 5:11; John 1:37).

Time is an important concept throughout the Bible. The New Testament uses two Greek words, *chronos* and *kairos*, that are both translated by the single English word "time." You may guess the meaning of the word *chronos* since it forms our word *chronology*—as in dates on a calendar. And another word for a wristwatch is *chronometer*, so it's no surprise that *chronos* means measured, tick-tock, clock and calendar time. Chronos time is always the same; it moves by with regularity and sometimes with boredom. Here's an example of chronos time: A teacher walked into her first-grade class and was surprised to find a boy standing there poking his stomach out. She asked, "Why are you poking your tummy out?" He replied, "Well, I had a stomachache and wanted to go home, but the school nurse gave me some medicine and said that I should just stick it out 'til lunch."

We experience the measured, relentless plodding of chronos time when we're "sticking it out," waiting for the school bell to ring, or when we're on the job and it's

Friday at 4:50 p.m., or when we have a batch of freshly baked brownies cooling and we have to wait thirty minutes before we can eat them. That's chronos time. Neurotics are painfully stuck in chronos time.

The other word for time, *kairos*, refers to "the right time," a special moment when everything comes together perfectly; a memorable experience that strikes us in a powerful way; or an instant of overwhelming insight from God. Kairos is *God's time*, the moment when God is trying to tell us something special or fulfill His plan. Are you receptive to God's timing, God's kairos?

To receive a kairos moment, we must break loose from the clock-watching busyness of life and create space for God's time. We must pace our lives so that kairos occasions don't sneak past unnoticed. Let me share some of my very personal kairos moments.

One was the birth of our first daughter, Melissa. It began in chronos time on August 9, 1989, as my wife, Diana, and I anxiously, painstakingly waited for her body to go through the necessary physiological changes in preparation for delivery. Once Diana moved into full-fledged labor, chronos time became irrelevant. We were caught up in the power and emotion (and especially for her, the pain) of the event. Before we knew it, hours had gone by, and for a brief moment, we were back in chronos time. We had realized that 8/9/89 would be a cute and convenient birth date for our daughter, but there were minor complications in getting Diana to the delivery room, the doctor was otherwise occupied and delayed, and we noticed that midnight was approaching. Soon it was 12:04 a.m. on 8/10/89, and thus the cute birth date had eluded us. Instantly we were over that trivial letdown and clicked back into kairos time. All that mattered now was the indescribable joy of receiving our beautiful, tiny miracle, Melissa. Clock time had stopped. We were in the midst of life's greatest moment. The air smelled sweeter, the colors were more vibrant, our hearts pounded with excitement and love. The nine months of waiting and worrying; the anxiety of labor; watching my wife suffer; the blood, sweat, and tears were all placed into proper perspective as my wife and I held our firstborn together, looked into her beautiful eyes, and felt that inimitable recognition: "This is our baby." It was a mystical experience of God's love mixed with human love.

Sometimes a kairos moment is when we experience the hilarity and joy of life. For me, there is joy in discovering humor in the midst of trouble. I was once in a traveling rock band. We had a large cargo truck that carried our equipment, but it was rather dilapidated. One time when one of our crew members, Lonnie, and I were driving to a performance in Birmingham, Alabama, we had a fuel pump go out, got that fixed, and had a flat tire. About an hour later, we had *another* flat! As the deadline for our concert approached, we became more and more stressed out. We had finally made it into downtown Birmingham with just a few minutes to spare before our gig, when the bearings in the steering wheel gearbox went out completely in city traffic. With all my might, I could not turn the wheel. Lonnie was over six feet tall and all muscle. He jumped from the passenger's seat and grabbed the big steering wheel with me. Together, with all our strength, the two of us managed to turn the wheel and steer the truck through traffic. It must have been a comic sight to see two guys steering a truck together, and sure enough, a big, burly trucker pulled up beside us at a light and yelled, "Hey, if you sissies can't drive a truck, park it!" Lonnie and I, on the verge of a nervous breakdown, then had a kairos moment. We realized how absurd we must have appeared, and we laughed so hard at ourselves that we nearly wrecked. Ultimately we made it to the gig on time, and I learned an important lesson: When things go wrong, look for the humor in the moment.

Kairos moments are often like that, a time when we see ourselves as we truly are. Sometimes humorously, other times seriously. A kairos moment may even be a time of judgment and self-conviction. If we watch for such moments, they can bring about confession, penitence, and growth.

One such moment exposed my selfishness. Years ago I was at a beach with a group of friends, including my brother. Without thinking, I walked across his nice clean blanket to fetch something, tracking sand. When I returned, I subconsciously avoided the sandy spot I had created and sat down on a clean spot. My brother pointed out my selfishness. "Lance, you tracked up the blanket and now you expect someone else to sit in your dirt!" Well, I hadn't done it intentionally, but as I stared at my sandy footprints on the blanket, I had a kairos moment. Those dirty footprints were a stark picture of my subconscious selfishness, my thoughtlessness. I was judged, not by my brother, but by my own footprints. That was one of many small but memorable events that led up to my conversion. It may seem insignificant, but I will never forget it.

Have you had moments when you were caught in your own selfishness? It may not feel good at the time, but in retrospect, I hope it made you a better person—and thus was a blessing.

Kairos moments usually are blessed times of revelation or insight, when the truth or beauty of life breaks through to us. We've all had those meaningful moments—watching a sunset or a child playing—and felt a deep, divine joy in God's creation.

God is a God of miraculous timing. He can see every era and epoch at once; the Lord stands at once in the past, the present, *and* the future. Yet while God is not *bound* by time, He has *chosen* to work within the confines of history. God is a God of calendars and seasons; His plans are specifically tied to proper moments, auspicious days, and perfect timing. The Bible speaks often about the "time being fulfilled" and the right time for events. Ecclesiastes 3:1 famously reminds us, "There is a time for everything, and a season for every activity under heaven." I particularly like the way the Amplified Bible renders verse 11: "He [God] also has planted eternity in men's hearts and minds [a divinely implanted sense of a purpose working through the ages]." God has a purpose for us, and when we get our timing in sync with His, great things can happen.

Are you receiving the kairos moments in your life? Are you making room for God to speak to you? Or are you stuck in chronos time, pointlessly ticking off the minutes, reeling in the years? Don't let life's best moments and messages pass by unnoticed. Don't be a clock watcher—be a *kairos watcher*. Live in the now. Seize the day!

MISTAKE NUMBER FOUR

"I FEEL LIKE I'M THE CENTER OF THE UNIVERSE"

Mistake Number Four
"I Feel Like I'm the Center of the Universe"

Our culture is commonly thrilled but rarely
fulfilled. Our society is lavishly entertained but scantily
content. Many Americans are indiscriminately rich but
selectively generous. We are, as social critic Christopher
Lasch put it, a "culture of narcissism."

The dictionary defines narcissism as "self-love;
excessive interest in one's own appearance, comfort,
importance," etc. I call it a "love affair with mirrors."
Excessive self-interest is the bane of modern American
life. And yet there is nothing new about hedonism. Go
back in time with me to the golden age of Greece. The
Athenians had a society very similar to ours. They were
highly civilized, with impressive architecture, art, music,
and even technology. Like many American cities, Athens
was cosmopolitan—a melting pot of peoples and religions.
And they had, like us, a leisure class. In fact, it was Greek
society that coined the term *hedonism*, a philosophical
movement that named personal pleasure as the chief goal
in life.

However, even as Hellenistic society began to
corrode by its own luxury, indulgence, and immorality,

other voices rose against the din, critics of their own
excess. Long before the apostle Paul came and preached
on Mars Hill outside Athens, the wisest Greeks looked
to their own mythology for guidance. We, too, can learn
from the best of their wisdom, as Paul himself used
Greek mythology as a bridge to bring the Athenians to
Christianity.

Consider the familiar Greek fable of Narcissus.
Narcissus was an extremely handsome young man who was
loved by a girl named Echo. But Echo's love for Narcissus
was unrequited; he was so vainly in love with himself that
he could not return Echo's love.

The Greek gods decided to punish Narcissus for
his rejection of Echo—with a most fitting punishment. He
came upon a reflecting pool and gazed admiringly at his
own image. He became so transfixed by his own vanity
that he stared at his own face for hours, stuck by the
water's edge, and the gods cast a spell upon him. He began
to grow roots out of his feet, became stuck by the pool
permanently, and turned into a flower—which is where the
beautiful narcissus blossom gets its name!

The myth is rather profound at several levels. First,
the Narcissus story is where we get the word *narcissism*.
But it also shares the same Greek root word, *narke*,
from which we get the word *narcotic*. *Narke* was Greek
for "numbness, stupor." Fittingly, Narcissus fell into a
narcotic stupor induced by his own egomania.

The Bible is filled with examples of narcissists:
the Egyptian pharaoh who sacrificed his firstborn son

rather than swallow his pride; King Saul, who was more concerned with popularity and praise than with what was best for the nation of Israel; King Nebuchadnezzar of Babylon, who built an immense statue to himself and forced everyone to worship his likeness; the vainglorious King Solomon, who late in life confessed, "Vanity, vanity, all is vanity."

In the New Testament, the woman at the well is a perfect example. Her conversation with Jesus can be understood as a metaphor for the plague of narcissism. Daily she came to the well obsessively because she was thirsty—not just for water but also for inner satisfaction. It is implied that she came there to meet men. She had gone from one lover to another, trying to find fulfillment.

And such is the human condition. We bounce from one craving to another—from hunger to longing to addiction, never finding fulfillment in ourselves and yet continuing to bow down at the altar of self-pleasure, the idol of Narcissus.

Peyton Conway March wrote a great truth: "There is a wonderful. . .law of nature that the three things we crave most in life—happiness, freedom, peace of mind— are always attained by giving them to someone else." It is a law of nature written into the fabric of the universe by our Creator, who is Himself the opposite of Narcissus. God is a God of caring and giving and sharing.

The woman at the well had not yet learned this truth. She had exhausted her physical hunt for happiness when she first encountered Jesus. But she realized He spoke a deep truth when He said, "Everyone who drinks this water will be thirsty again" (John 4:13). Physical satisfaction is fleeting. The long-term cure for the disease of narcissism is not physical but spiritual.

We should learn this truth simply by considering an obvious statistic: Over the last twenty years, personal affluence has increased greatly in the United States. Most Americans drive far nicer cars and live in much bigger homes than their parents did. Yet as the markers of luxury and affluence have risen, so has the suicide rate. If material things could quench and satiate our desires, then we should see the opposite result. Instead, we have a society that is learning, as Rabbi Harold Kushner put it, that "having everything is not enough."

Christopher Lasch was correct: We are a culture of narcissism, choking on selfishness and self-absorption. In our society, narcissus is not a flower, but a weed—a weed that grows in the garden of the soul. To amplify the metaphor, this is no ordinary weed. This is kudzu!

Throughout the Southeast, kudzu is thriving, and perhaps even winning the battle over pesticides and cultivators. Kudzu constantly needs cutting back. (By the way, do you know how to plant kudzu? Dig a two-inch hole, drop in the seed, and *run*!)

Like emotional kudzu, narcissism is rampant in America—and yes, I find it in the garden of my own soul. This raging self-centeredness requires eternal vigilance and constant trimming.

You may not think of yourself as self-centered or

narcissistic, because neurotics and codependents spend a great deal of energy worrying about other people. But an honest self-evaluation may reveal that much of your concern about other people is, deep down, a worry about what they think about *you*. In seeking to please others, you may be motivated less by Christian charity and more by your desire to make them approve of you as a person.

One mark of a neurotic is that if we see two people whispering, we think they are talking negatively about us! When someone calls my church office and tells me they have a concern they wish to discuss with me, it is usually the next day before my calendar is clear to meet with them. So for the next twenty-four hours, I fret about what their "concern" will be and become tense, having concluded that they must have a complaint against *me*. Typically, their "concern" turns out to be a personal problem for which they need my help. It had nothing to do with me, but the fact that I perceived it to concern me betrays my narcissistic neurosis. My self-preoccupation cuts me off from love and abundant living; narcissism makes me overly sensitive, overly defensive to critical comments, and less caring. I have had success in calming my nerves and bridling my childish selfishness by telling myself (sometimes aloud, when necessary), "They are not talking about me. I am *not* the center of the universe."

We all have egos. *Ego* is the Latin word for "I," and in Freudian psychology, it refers to the individual's conscious self-identity. God created the ego and has blessed each "I" with free moral choice, independent will and thought, and autonomy of being. But the blessing also has a curse: In our fallen nature, we usually turn inward, particularly under stress, and begin to put most of our energies into taking care of *self*.

Don't despair! In the eternal view, Narcissus shall not be triumphant. Jesus has waged a cosmic war against narcissism, and He invites you to join Him on the winning team. He said, "If anyone would come after me, he must deny himself and take up his cross and follow me" (Mark 8:34).

Speaking of the cross: Jesus battled Narcissus in the Garden of Gethsemane and on the hill of Golgotha. We don't understand the full mysteries of it. But in reading the account of Jesus' struggle in the garden, it seems that He was fighting against the very forces of selfishness and self-will that had previously reigned in human nature.

While we believe that Jesus was perfect—indeed, God in the flesh—He also had a human component. God had chosen to put on human flesh and immerse Himself in human society with all its frailties. And so Jesus felt the fallen state of mortal flesh and apparently even felt the pull of human selfish temptation as the devil tempted Him in the desert. In the Garden of Gethsemane, Jesus truly did battle with the fleshly desire to preserve Himself, to take care of number one, to put Himself first. But Love won out over Narcissus.

In the next chapter, we will consider the ways in which Jesus defeated Narcissus and how we can do the same.

SOLUTION NUMBER FOUR

"THEY ARE **NOT** TALKING ABOUT ME"

Solution Number Four
"They Are Not Talking about Me"

Highly sensitive people have a gift: a high-performance nervous system that helps us tune in to the feelings of others. We are caring and empathetic. The bad news is that the same tightly wound nervous system easily misfires. One small critical remark about us can trigger a cascade of neurotic thoughts. We quickly assume that people are talking negatively about us or that we don't measure up or that we are constantly being examined and gossiped about.

I am suggesting that people are, 99 percent of the time, not wasting their energy attacking you or me. The solution to many of our problems begins when we routinely remind ourselves: "They are not talking about me!" Make this your mantra—say it aloud if necessary. Your subconscious mind needs to be told, out loud, what your rational, conscious mind understands. But perhaps your conscious mind needs to be thoroughly convinced first. Read on.

As a minister, I move from parish to parish, which affords me a detachment and 20/20 hindsight of relationships in my past. I discovered that even those who seemed to be enemies did not rejoice when I moved away. They did not harbor ill feelings toward me—in fact, they had an overall positive opinion of me. That is not to say I had merely imagined their complaints, attacks, or moments of dissatisfaction with me. But I had clearly blown these things out of proportion.

Even the toxic, negative complainers who may disapprove of some aspect of my personality generally move on to another concern or topic very quickly. If nothing else, they have other people to gripe about! Compared to the hours of sleepless tossing and turning I wasted in analyzing their passing complaints about me, they never spent a fraction of their energy worrying about Lance Moore.

Because the core of this unfounded worry stems from our self-centeredness, the solution requires that we confess our narcissism and begin to be quieter persons who truly listen before jumping to conclusions about what people are actually saying. If we wish to be free of neurosis, a key step is to kill Narcissus. In psychological terms, Narcissus stands for our false, fragile, inflated egos. But it takes more than good psychology to outwit our inner foe. Narcissism is a spiritual illness that requires a spiritual cure.

Consider how Jesus defeated Narcissus. First, after hours in painful prayer, even to the point of sweating blood, He said to God the Father, "Yet not what I will, but what you will" (Mark 14:36). Next, Jesus offered His very life as the ultimate sacrifice on the cross, the ultimate denial of self—the temporary death of God the Son! Something powerful and mysterious happened in the universe. Narcissus was defeated. The dark spirits of pagan mythology, along with the dark impulses of the human soul, were trampled. Jesus was victorious.

Christ's victory is not just a footnote in history. He invites us to be a part of the winning side. Publishers Clearinghouse, the magazine distributor known for its sweepstakes, mails out an envelope announcing, "You may already be a winner!" Of course, the odds are more likely that you're a loser in their sweepstakes. But in the bigger scheme of eternity, you are indeed already a winner in Christ. Through God's spiritual power given to us through Christ, we can win out over the dark forces of evil within us and without.

Why, then, do we still act like losers? Why do we live in fear? It is because we have not fully accepted the power of victorious love. First John 4:18 tells us that love drives out fear. (Again, I turn to the writings of Saint John for advice. This should not come as a surprise. John was an expert on love: He wrote the famous words, "God is love," and called himself "the disciple whom Jesus loved.") John calls us to embrace the beauty and wonder and power and joy of unconditional love.

Sadly, some people have never tasted even a morsel of true love. Maybe you've only known cheap imitations—flawed impostors—of love. Maybe your most intimate relationships—with your parents, spouse, or best friends—have been scarred by manipulation, deceit, and self-interest.

That is why both John and Paul focus on the cross in their discussion of love. Here is a symbol of true love, love that is selfless and free, no strings attached. And yet it's more than a mere symbol; it's a means. Christ on the cross is not only an emblem of love, not just the evidence of hope: Christ crucified is the very essence and energy for all that love can be in us. I'll put it this way: What more could God do to demonstrate His love for you? Or as Jesus put it, "Greater love has no one than this, that he lay down his life for his friends" (John 15:13).

In 1873, a Belgian Catholic priest named Joseph Damien De Veuster was sent to minister to lepers on the Hawaiian Island of Molokai. He tried hard to build friendships among the lepers, but wherever he turned, they shunned him. It seemed as if every door was closed. Each Sunday he preached about love, but no one seemed to listen. No one responded to his ministry. After years of futile effort, Father Damien reluctantly made the decision to leave. Dejected, he made his way to the docks to board a ship to take him back to Belgium. As he stood on the dock recounting his ineffective ministry among the lepers, he then noticed some numbness in his hands. When he looked down at them, he discovered some mysterious white spots on his skin. With terror, he realized immediately that he had contracted leprosy—whereupon he returned to the leper colony and resumed his ministry. Word of his disease spread quickly through the colony, and hundreds of lepers soon gathered outside his hut. They understood his pain, fear, and uncertainty about the future. On the following

Sunday, as Father Damien arrived at the chapel, he found hundreds of worshipers there. The service was standing room only, with more gathered outside the chapel. His ministry had become enormously successful. The reason? He was one of them now. He understood and empathized with them. And most of all, he had proved his love to the point of risking death. There is no greater love.

In a sense, this is what God has done for us. Christ came into our "leper colony," our disease-ridden world, took upon Himself our infirmities, and loved us even unto death. What more can God do to demonstrate unconditional love? And He returned from the dead with new flesh, transformed and purified. Thomas could touch Christ's body—Jesus still had the human component; He had not rejected physical creation. But Christ had transformed our frail condition into a new creature.

We, too, can be transfigured into new creatures, post-Narcissans, kingdom servants, creatures of our God and King. While we shall not know that full and final transformation until—through death—we are changed into heavenly beings, we can catch glimpses of it now. Jesus said the kingdom is within us. In essence, He told the woman at the well that by worshiping God "in spirit and in truth," we can transcend our obsessions and addictions and find peace. Through Christ's victory over selfishness, we can occasionally rise above our fallen natures.

It is not enough to focus on our own personal victory. To fully defeat Narcissus, we should seek to invite all who will come to join the winning team and include everyone in the victory party. The best way to break out of a fixation on our own troubles is to resolve to be encouragers of others. Rooting others on to victory is a key to happiness, as well as the right thing to do.

Be an encourager. From a selfish standpoint, the best thing about being an encourager is that it helps us, as well. This has even been clinically proven by a team of psychologists who ran a test. They divided a panel of volunteers at random into two groups. To hide the real meaning of the experiment, the volunteers were told they were involved in a test of facial muscles. One group was asked to frown for one hour, and the other group was instructed to smile. At the end of the hour, the subjects were evaluated as to their emotional mood and feelings of well-being. As you might suspect, the ones who had smiled were *significantly* happier than the ones who had frowned. So as you smile and encourage others, it is your own attitude that benefits the most!

In the writings of the apostle Paul, we find this message again and again, "Encourage one another." I think it's significant to note that often he wrote these words from a prison cell. Words can be cheap, but some words are freighted with grand treasure and power because of the person and place from which they come. The rhetorical torrent that flows from the mouth of Al Sharpton as he lounges in his limousine, for example, does not carry nearly the same weight as Dr. Martin Luther King Jr.'s "Letter from the Birmingham Jail." In my seminary days, I was never as moved by the idle ponderings of ivory-tower theologians as I was by Dietrich Bonhoeffer's stark *Letters and Papers from Prison*, nobly written while he awaited execution as a Christian martyr in a Nazi prison. The voice of suffering is like thunder. So when Paul writes of joy and encouragement, he is not spewing mushy clichés and soft platitudes like some tenderfooted advice columnist. His words have gone through the fiery trial; they have been hammered on the anvil of affliction. He gets our attention—or should, anyway.

The truth is, in our complacent, middle-class existence, we rarely listen to Paul, because we are too preoccupied with our own petty whining. We are deeply concerned because the cable TV has gone out or the newspaper was late or we spilled coffee in the car or a telemarketer has interrupted our supper. Such momentous calamities! Much of the time we just don't have enough genuine, serious trouble in life to make us pause and drink from the soothing well of scripture.

Of course, on September 11, 2001, America had its illusions of comfort and safety shattered. Times such as these are when we hear Paul's words with new ears: He is telling us of the absolute importance of being there for one another in times of distress and trouble.

Other scriptures challenge us to go beyond just being there for our close friends. Jesus said, "You are the salt of the earth" (Matthew 5:13). Our duty as Christians, as the salt, the tasty flavor, is to be encouragers for the whole planet. We are the yeast of the whole batch, and whatever good rises in this world must first come from us. Our words should be uplifting in a downcast age. The church is to be in the business of spreading peace and joy. Paul affirmed the church in this. He wrote to Philemon and his church, "Your love has given me great joy and encouragement, because you, brother, have refreshed the hearts of the saints" (Philemon 7).

The letter to Philemon is one of the shortest books in the Bible but one of my favorites because it is filled with positivity and joy. Paul's love for Philemon in particular jumps off the page. Oh, how I love to be in the presence of a person who refreshes my heart! If you throw a party, all you need to do is invite one such person and your party will be a success. You know what kind of person I'm referring to: not the loud, obnoxious, lampshade-on-the-head guy; not the beauty queen who can only talk about herself; and not the whiner who can only complain that the *hors d'oeuvres* are cold. The refresher is the one who has a smile, who greets you as if he's truly glad to see you, who asks you how you are and then actually waits to receive your answer; the one who listens to your jokes without interrupting; and most of all, the one who steers the conversation to things pleasant and substantial rather than ugly gossip or the all-too-often discourse of running down the people who did not attend the party. Philemon must have been such a person. Apparently he was instrumental in starting a home church. We can imagine that people looked forward to going to church because Philemon would be there to greet them at the door with a big smile and a warm handshake. Moreover, we find in this passage an interesting story if we read between the lines. Apparently Philemon's young slave, Onesimus, had been an uncooperative, useless servant. We believe that he had, understandably, rebelled and run away from his enslavement and somehow managed to find Philemon's friend, Paul, in Rome. Rather than having him arrested, Paul adopted Onesimus like a son. He became his tutor. You can imagine that after being adopted and tutored by the irrepressible, upbeat Paul, the young man was transformed from lazy rebel into a productive, happy Christian. And then, ironically, Onesimus became a slave again—a slave by choice, a servant to Jesus and His church. Yes, Paul could have said to Onesimus, "You no-good, worthless outlaw. You failed as a slave, so now you can rot in prison. I'm turning you in to the authorities." Instead, Paul, the original positive thinker with a refreshing, forgiving heart, embraced the former slave and set him free, both literally and figuratively. That is the power of words of encouragement.

This letter to Philemon is filled with irony. Paul was the one who was in chains. Paul had every right to complain. If I had written that letter from prison, it would have gone something like this:

> Philemon,
>
> I'm stuck here in prison. It is freez-ing at night, I'm hungry, and the last thing I need is your runaway slave bothering me and looking for a father figure. I don't really

want to hear about how wonderful things
are going for you and your church. Send me
food and blankets, not letters.

>Your unhappy, miserable,
>and cold friend,
>Lance

But of course, that is not what we have in Paul's
letter. Instead, we have the apostle proclaiming the love of
Christ, thanking Philemon for his work, encouraging the
church, converting a slave boy, and expressing gratitude for
the joy that they have given him in the midst of his suffering.

Words of comfort are obviously vital for people
who are suffering. Words of encouragement can also be
very important in the good times, when everything seems
to be going well for our friends. Life is like an iceberg.
Much of the distress, anxiety, and worries in the lives of
our friends lurks below the waterline, unseen.

I am fortunate. As a pastor, I get to peek beneath
the surface, I get more opportunities to help folks in
trouble, and I have more chances to see how the principle
of encouragement can be life changing. I remember once,
early in my ministry, I received a call late in the evening.
The young woman's voice on the phone sounded full of
stress. I'll call her Jane. She said, "Reverend Moore, you
probably don't know me. . .my name is Jane. I've only
attended your church a few times. But I'm upset and I
really need to talk to someone. My husband was killed in
a plane crash a few months ago, and instead of getting

better about it, I'm feeling worse. I don't have any kinfolk here; I have no one to turn to." Well, it was nearly 10 p.m. and I was extremely hesitant to go by myself to the home of a single woman—a stranger—leaving my wife at home with a newborn baby to contend with, so I suggested to Jane that she come to my office first thing in the morning. But she insisted that she really needed to talk to someone that night. Sensing my hesitation, she added that her two children would be there, as well. Something in the tone of her voice told me that I needed to respond to this plea for help. So I left the comfort of my recliner and drove to Jane's home, held her little girl in my arms, and spent about an hour mostly listening to Jane's troubles and grief. In the weeks ahead, I referred her to a Christian psychologist, and over time she got better.

Several years later, I bumped into her psychologist, who said: "Lance, now that she's happy and healthy, I think you ought to know something about Jane. She told me that the night she called you, she was in deep depression. She had a bottle of sleeping pills by her bed and had decided to take her life. She had made a deal with the Lord: She would make one phone call, one last cry for help—and if you had simply dismissed her as a crank call, she would have killed herself."

I did not tell him how close I had come to putting her off.

It is an indescribable joy to learn that you have saved another human's life. But if you are a habitual encourager, you may have saved a life without even knowing it. Yes, sometimes people are clinging to the end of their rope and we can't see it. Sometimes their desperation is purposely well-hidden behind smiles and the quick exchange of "How ya doin'?" "I'm doin' great." Paul's challenge to us to be encouragers, to refresh each other's hearts, are not words merely for a season. They are essential commands for a *lifetime*, for every day, for every circumstance. If we make a habit of being encouragers rather than whiners, who knows how many lives we can touch? We will probably never know the times when one kind word from our lips has saved a sinking soul, when the Lord was counting on us to be the ones to throw a lifeline to someone drowning in despondency.

Our hymns often echo Paul's sentiments about the value of encouragement. Consider the well-beloved song "Rescue the Perishing." It was written by someone who had far more right to grumble in life than I do: Fanny Crosby. She had been blinded by an incompetent doctor at six weeks of age yet was the most prolific hymn writer in America. She wrote more than eight thousand upbeat hymns, including this one:

> *Down in the human heart, crushed by the tempter,*
> *Feelings lie buried that grace can restore;*
> *Touched by a loving heart, wakened by kindness,*
> *Chords that were broken will vibrate once more.*
> *Rescue the perishing, care for the dying,*
> *Jesus is merciful, Jesus will save.*

About her blindness, Fanny Crosby said, "It seemed intended by the blessed providence of God that I should be blind all my life, and I thank Him for the dispensation. If perfect earthly sight were offered me tomorrow, I would not accept it. I might not have sung hymns to the praise of God if I had been distracted by the beautiful and interesting things about me." Her tombstone is inscribed with her famous lyrics, "Blessed assurance, Jesus is mine. Oh, what a foretaste of glory divine."

If you do not know how to be an encourager, get a hymnal. Many of the songwriters endured hardships in life not unlike those of Paul, yet they proclaimed the joy of the Christian life louder than I ever will. Their words were alloyed in the fiery crucible of anguish but were poured out as refined gold, as testimony to the triumphant joy of the Christian faith. How can we sing these holy words and not *mean* them, not adopt them as our daily mantra, our *modus vivendi*, our "way of living"? How can we read the scriptures, written in the blood of the martyrs, or sing our hymns and creeds, wrung from the hearts of the saints, and persist in being whiners, pessimists, critics, naysayers, and, well, party poopers?

Join the mighty procession, the victorious throng of rejoicing saints trailing across the centuries from Philemon's refreshing church and Paul's prison cell to the hymn writer's pen, and become, like them, *encouragers*!

If you accept the assignment of being an encourager, you have broken out of narcissism. Any gesture, no matter how small, that is focused on others rather than on yourself, drives a stake through the dark heart of Narcissus. Let me share an example of how even the most trivial act can achieve this. A friend of mine had in her hand a package of three gourmet chocolates that she had just purchased for herself. She had eaten one, and if she had the chocolate addiction I suffer, she would have hungrily devoured the other two pieces. Instead, she gave one piece to me and one piece to another bystander. She gave it without us requesting it, without compulsion. And the striking thing was her casual comment as she gave us the majority of her candy: "This was so good, I just had to share it."

That may seem like a meager thing. I call attention to it as a perfect example of what you and I can do every day: defeat narcissism in small ways, piece by piece, moment by moment. Narcissus says, "This is so good, I want it all for myself." God says, "This is so good, I want to share it."

The great secret of life is this: *Anything good is better when shared.* Think about it. When you have good news, what's your first instinct? To pick up the phone and call someone to share your good news! Why can't we be that way with everything, including our time and money? Isn't it much more fun to watch a movie or eat a fine meal with a friend than alone? Isn't laughter doubly delicious when others laugh with us? Everything good is better when shared. Especially love.

One of my favorite children's songs is "Magic Penny." Some of the lyrics are as follows:

Love is something
if you give it away, give it away. . .
    you end up having more.
It's just like a magic penny,
    hold it tight and you won't have any.
Lend it, spend it, and you'll have so many,
    they'll roll all over the floor.

Giving love away and sharing our good things with others is the secret to defeating Narcissus. Our charity does as much for us as it does for others. In the process of sharing, life is enriched. This is why Jesus died on the cross, so that we might find a life beyond self-centeredness—a life of shared joy and deep contentment, which comes from sacrifice and service. Jesus said, "Whoever wants to save his life will lose it, but whoever loses his life for me and for the gospel will save it" (Mark 8:35).

That is a secret, a truth, so good, I just had to share it!

MISTAKE NUMBER FIVE

"I MAKE SIMPLE THINGS TOO COMPLICATED"

Mistake Number Five
"I Make Simple Things Too Complicated"

Simple is better. It's just that simple! It took me forty years to learn that truth. For most of my life, I was guilty of "Einsteinism"—of being overly cognitive, trying to turn simple questions into a Unified Field Theory of quantum physics. If you are trying to split the atom, having the brains of Albert Einstein is a plus. But for daily living, ignorance is bliss. I began to learn this years ago when my friend Gerald and I listened to another friend, Mark, as he sought counsel regarding his terrible life situation. Mark had lost his job. It was a miserable job of low pay and hard, unskilled labor, but Mark was devastated nonetheless. To compound his woes, Mark and his girlfriend had an argument, Mark lost his cool, and they broke up. Mark was in tears, spiraling into the paralysis of deep depression.

After Mark shared his troubles, I began to slip into my Freudian psychology mode to formulate a detailed plan of therapy for Mark, to save him from depression. Before I could begin to share my profound pontifications, Gerald looked Mark straight in the eye and said with bold, matter-of-fact confidence: "Mark, here's what you do. Tomorrow you go down to the unemployment office and you find a job. You are a nice, friendly fellow with a strong back, and you'll have no problem finding an even better job than the one you had. Your girlfriend, on the other hand, is irreplaceable. She is the best gal you can ever hope for. So you go buy some roses and you head straight over to her house and tell her you're sorry. Even if it was her fault. And quit worrying about any of this, because in a few days, things will be better."

Mark instantly brightened up. In the coming days, he did exactly what Gerald had instructed him to do. He landed a much better job, he married the girl, and they lived happily ever after. I'm not making this up. It really happened, and to this day, Mark should be thankful that I never got a chance to share with him my highly cerebral, thoughtful, and ridiculously intricate plan for his future!

Highly sensitive people tend to make life more complicated than it needs to be. Yes, existence is complex, infinitely so. But that is the point. Our brains are finite, our resources limited, and we have only a few waking hours each day, so we have to reduce the millions of possibilities down to a handful of reasonable, doable choices. The most successful life is the simple one. Intelligent minds can understand this, but at the same time, the more intelligent we are the more we tend to see the vast array of possibilities, the more we try to overanalyze, second-guess, reconsider, calculate—and, in the end, hesitate—to the point of inaction. Or at best, we scurry off in a hundred directions chasing irrelevant aims. Sometimes we need to stop and take a moment to ask, *What is the one thing most needful? What should be my priority? Why am I doing the things I do?*

A woman stood on a pier and watched a fisherman pull in a large fish, measure it, and throw it back. He caught a second fish, smaller this time; he measured it and put it in his bucket. Oddly, all the large fish that he caught that measured ten inches or more he discarded. All fish *smaller* than ten inches he kept. Puzzled, the woman asked, "Pardon me, but why do you keep the little ones and throw back the big ones?" The fisherman looked up and explained, "Simple—my frying pan measures only ten inches across."

For some people, the ten-inch frying pan represents their limited dreams and goals. For others, it might represent real physical, mental, and spiritual capacities. But most of us probably have more talent and capability than we have imagination; we often limit our own achievement because all we think we have is a ten-inch frying pan. Some of us need to *expand* our measure of success, and others need to totally *redefine* how they measure success.

Henry David Thoreau wrote: "Why should we be in such desperate haste to succeed, and in such desperate enterprises? If a man does not keep pace with his companions, perhaps it is because he hears a different drummer. Let him step to the music which he hears, however measured."

Sadly, most people measure success by the size of their bank accounts. There is a terrible problem in gauging your success by a dollar figure: What do you do if you reach old age and never acquire that amount of money? But worse yet, what if you *do* attain that amount of money at an early age? Does that mean that the remainder of your life has no meaning?

Tell me if this man was a success or a failure: When he was seven years old, his family was forced out of their home on a legal technicality. His mother died when he was nine, so he had to work to help support the family even while just a child. At twenty-two, he lost his job as a store clerk. He wanted to go to law school, but his education wasn't good enough. At twenty-three, he went into debt to become a partner in a small store. At twenty-six, his business partner died, leaving him a huge debt that took years to repay. At twenty-eight, after courting a girl for four years, he asked her to marry him. She said no! At thirty-seven, on his third try, he was elected to Congress, but two years later, he failed to be reelected. Finally, he did marry, but his wife became mentally ill. At forty-one, his four-year-old son died. At forty-five, he ran for the Senate and lost. At forty-seven, he failed as a vice presidential candidate. At forty-nine, he ran for the Senate again, and lost. He was so hated by thousands of people that he was killed in his fifties by one of his enemies.

Was this man a success or a failure? If I told you that his name was Abraham Lincoln, perhaps the greatest president we've ever had, you might be quick to change your opinion. Obviously, he was a success. But suppose he had *lost* the presidency? Would you then dismiss him as a failure? No, he would have still been a great man for two reasons: He never gave up, and he loved God and loved his neighbors with all his might. And that is the only true measure of success: How much have you loved?

I have observed this quirk of human nature play itself out most clearly in the business world. The brainy intellectual who is voted "most likely to succeed" in high school rarely ends up fulfilling the prophecy. (Microsoft tycoon Bill Gates is the exception that proves the rule.) Most intellectuals spend four years in college struggling to narrow their choice of majors in time to make it into a specific graduate school. By contrast, the most successful small-business owners and entrepreneurs I have known are smart but not straight-A students. The effective ones have zeroed in on a task, focused on a particular niche market, and worked diligently without distraction until they turned a profit. Even our "exception to the rule," Bill Gates, began his career with one specific, clear objective: He developed an effective operating system for IBM computers. Yes, after he became wealthy, he hired other great minds to develop many diverse types of software, but his initial success came from a single product.

Some personalities seem committed to turning mundane activities into high drama. A trip to the store requires careful planning and deliberation. Frenetic energies are devoted to choosing which restaurant for lunch. And when an actual difficulty arises in one's relationships, it becomes, for the neurotic, an all-consuming worry bordering on panic. Perhaps there is an adrenaline rush to be had in living at the edge of hysteria, but life does not usually call for such an exaggerated approach to daily routine. The great secret is that most problems in life resolve themselves if left alone long enough. As the Beatles said, let it be. But the highly sensitive person is never hands-off. You will never hear the words *que sera, sera* or *laissez-faire* come from our lips.

The New Testament includes a compelling example of such a hyperneurotic personality in action. Two sisters, Mary and Martha, opened their home to Jesus and His followers. Jesus began to teach. Martha frantically ran about the house, "'worried and upset about many things'" (Luke 10:41), but Mary sat quietly at the feet of Jesus to listen to His wisdom. Jesus affirmed Mary's quiet devotion as "the one thing needful." There is a time for action, but to sit at the feet of Jesus for listening and learning is a number one priority. In other moments, "the one thing needful" may vary, but the principle remains the same: Instead of being distracted and "busy at many things," settle on the one thing most pressing in the moment and give yourself to it. Martha did nothing wrong. In fact, from her perspective, taking care of the housework and showing concern about her guest's comfort were more important than sitting around. From our perspective, however, to be in the same room with Jesus would be a fantastic, once-in-a-lifetime opportunity. Martha tried to make the simple gathering of friends, for the purpose of being with the Great Teacher, into a fretful, complicated, big production.

Letting go of the complexities in our lives is difficult because it involves letting go of control. Or maybe the truth is that we are not as much in control as we think we are. Let go of the illusion that you are in control and of the delusion that you need to be in control. I'm not one for cutesy clichés, but here's an aphorism that neurotics should live by: "Let go and let God!"

SOLUTION NUMBER FIVE

"I WILL **SIMPLY EMBRACE** OPPORTUNITY"

Solution Number Five
"I Will Simply Embrace Opportunity"

Life is indeed filled with complexities. Nevertheless, the most successful people are not always the smartest people; nor are they, by nature, consumed with juggling multifarious details. They have simply learned three things: (1) Keep it simple, stupid (the famous KISS acronym); (2) be positive and practical; (3) embrace opportunity.

Everyone loves a good opportunity. But few understand the difference between opportunity and luck. The person who takes advantage of possibilities is *smart*, not lucky. So-called lucky breaks come to all of us, and over a lifetime, I suspect we all have about an equal amount of opportunities. The person we call lucky is more than likely just a person whose eyes are open to possibilities and who has said yes to his or her opportunities.

Let me illustrate by telling one of Aesop's fables, the one entitled "The Traveler and Fortune." A traveler wearied from a long journey sat down, overcome with fatigue, on the very brink of a deep well. Just as he was about to doze off and fall off the edge into the water, Dame

Fortune, whom we sometimes call Lady Luck, appeared to the traveler and woke him from his slumber. Lady Luck said, "Good sir, pray wake up: For if you fall into the well, the blame will be thrown on me, and I shall be given a bad name among mortals; for I find that men are sure to impute their calamities to me, however much by their own folly they have really brought them on themselves."

And the moral of the fable, Aesop concluded, is that "everyone is more or less master of his own fate." We like to blame bad luck for *our* bad choices. We fail to recognize that opportunities taken are not so much good fortune as they are good choices. Persistence, perseverance, and boldness in grasping opportunity are keys to success in all endeavors.

Consider this true success story. One particular product started out as Mr. Pemberton's Triple-X Liver Pills. But that didn't sell, so he made it a cough syrup and called it Dr. Pemberton's Glove of Flower Cough Syrup. Actually he wasn't a doctor at all, but a druggist. Then he worked on a hangover cure for a while in his basement. He put together the extracts of fruits and leaves and nuts, a touch of caffeine, and some sugar to cut the bitter taste. All you had to do was add some water, drink it, and it would help ease the pain of a hangover. Then one day one of his fellow pharmacists accidentally added some carbonated water to it instead of regular water, and it tasted wonderful. A new product was born that has since made billions of dollars—a drink called Coca-Cola! Yes, the accidental addition of carbonated water was a touch of good fortune, but behind it all was the diligence of Mr. Pemberton. More to the point, it was the Woodruff family who later saw the great opportunity in the product and, with hard work and clever marketing, turned it into a huge success. And that is not the end of the story. The Woodruffs, with all their millions, saw another opportunity: They began to pour Coca-Cola money into a small college in Atlanta called Emory. It has become one of the best universities in the South. Literally millions and millions of dollars have built Emory's beautiful campus and funded its sterling academics and research. . .all because of a simple product, Coke.

So examine your life honestly and ask, "Have I had bad luck, or have I made bad choices? Do I make life so overcomplicated that the obvious opportunities pass me by? When opportunity knocks, do I open every door except the correct one?" It is smart to stay on the lookout for material opportunities; like the Woodruffs, we should also be on the lookout for times when we can serve God and do good in the world. These opportunities, too, come to us more often than we answer. I will confess that for much of my life I kept looking for some grandiose way to change the world, missing the simple daily opportunities to do good.

Paul Harvey told the true story of a young man who was able to look beyond himself to find ways to help others. The teenager was busy at his job of carrying out the groceries for a local supermarket. Something drew his attention to a woman in the parking lot who was struggling with her groceries. Her cart was full of bags and packages, and so were her arms. His path back to the store took him in her direction. Walking toward her, he watched as she put one of her bundles on the roof of the car in order to dig her car keys out of her purse. Then she began to load her packages from her shopping cart into the backseat. Before the young man reached her, she was already cranking up and driving off—forgetting to retrieve the package she'd placed on the roof. We've all done that. Now the grocery boy was closer to the car, so he began to run after her. As the car turned, the bundle on the roof slid off. Fortunately, the young man caught the package just before it hit the pavement. To his pleasant surprise, he had not just saved a worthless bundle of blankets; wrapped inside was the woman's beautiful little baby!

It's not every day that one is given an opportunity to be a hero! Or is it? How many tragedies reported in the local news might instead have been a story of heroism or sacrificial good deeds if only someone had simply taken the opportunity to help? How many times daily do we, in our self-centered dullness, walk obliviously past someone in need? How many opportunities to change the world do we miss in a lifetime?

Consider this: Even life's problems present an opportunity. Even in the midst of a terrible crisis, God can bring opportunity. When we say the word *crisis*, we usually think of catastrophe, calamity, something awful. That's not all the word means. As I reported in my previous book, *Outdoors with God*, the dictionary defines it as "a turning point for good *or* bad." In the original Greek, the word *crisis* came from the word for decision or judgment. In Chinese, the symbol for *crisis* is also the symbol for *opportunity*. So a crisis is, literally, an opportunity for positive change. When we are faced with what may appear to be a calamity, we must decide whether we will turn it for good or for evil.

I am writing these words just twenty-four hours after my community was hit by a major hurricane. Ivan, a massive category 4 storm, has wreaked havoc on homes and businesses, including my own home's roof. As I survey the damage, it makes me question my own words. How can such a tragedy ever be an opportunity for something good? I reflect back to exactly twenty-five years ago, when Gulf Shores, Alabama, just twenty minutes from where I now live, was hit by a similar storm, Hurricane Frederick. It turned out to be the start of an economic boom in this county, thanks to a combination of federal aid, new attention to the area, and an opening of beachfront real estate to development. That is not to make light of the tragedy, particularly the lives lost. That is not to say that the good outweighs the bad. I am merely pointing out that when tragedy strikes, something of value can be pulled from the wreckage.

Also in my state of Alabama, in the town of Enterprise, a monument stands as testimony to the principal of disaster being turned into opportunity and "good fortune." The monument is a statue of a bug! In the middle of the town square is the famous Boll Weevil Monument. Many years ago, when agriculture was the core of the economy, the townspeople erected it in honor of the pest that destroyed their cotton crops. With their cotton crops doing poorly, they turned to planting peanuts. Another Alabamian, George Washington Carver, had discovered myriad ways to use peanuts and encouraged South Alabamians to plant the crop. It thrived and proved to be more profitable than cotton.

Sometimes fortune doesn't present itself in any form, good or bad. Sometimes opportunity does not knock. Then you have to go out your door and track it down! If you are having bad luck, make your own good luck. Here are some pragmatic tips to help you create your own opportunities:

1. Pick your battles. You can't do it all. A common mistake young entrepreneurs make is to overshoot. They want to conquer the world, forgetting that even Alexander the Great started with a small battle, then the conquest of a small country, before trying to rule the world. If you must have delusions of grandeur, focus on a single "delusion" and prove your prowess with a laserlike focus on success in one part of your life or vocation. A sure sign of maturity is when we properly assess what we can and cannot do.

2. Find a mentor. I was stubborn as a youth. I tried to learn everything and

do everything myself. It is much simpler and quicker to find a wise, experienced mentor and tap his or her brain. Usually people enjoy sharing (showing off!) their skill, talent, and knowledge—you simply need to ask them. An obvious example would be learning how to use a computer. Do it yourself if you wish: You can read a five-hundred-page manual on Microsoft Windows and another five-hundred-page manual for your word processor. Or you can spend weeks of trial and error, mousing and clicking away, and if you are lucky enough not to do damage to your system software, you will eventually figure out how to operate the computer. On the other hand, if you can find a friend who already has been using that type of computer and software, in thirty minutes he or she can impart a year's worth of trial-and-error knowledge. This commonsense example also applies to less technical fields and to life in general.

Finding a teacher/mentor is such an obvious time-saver, why do we so rarely employ this principle? Because we are prideful and stubborn—which leads to our third tip.

3. Foster humility and team spirit. Humility is not just an obligatory Christian virtue, it is a key to proper living. Humility brings right order to life. In humility, we discover that we cannot be all things to all people. In humility, we learn that other people have better skills at certain tasks, and thus we eagerly turn those tasks over to them. The conceited perfectionist who believes "if you want something done right, do it yourself," wonders why his schedule is always overwhelmed. Humility leads to delegation. Delegation frees people up for the tasks at which they excel. Delegation simplifies life and allows us to focus on the aspects of life we feel passionate about. And delegation is more than mere time management. It pushes us in the healthy direction of social interdependence. The old TEAM acronym is rich with truth: Together everyone achieves more. Being a team player does require a humble willingness to share the fruits and rewards of work. When the whole team wins, the trophy cannot sit on your mantel alone; but the chance of winning trophies increases exponentially with the number of team partners.

Outside of the paid workplace, how do you

assemble your team? Again, humility is the key. The sweet-spirited person attracts cooperative helpers like a magnet. People like to work with pleasant people who share credit. Volunteers are drawn to those who affirm and encourage them. The first time you ask people to help you but then proceed to diminish their esteem and dismiss their ability (by saying such things as, "There's a better way to do that. . ." or "What I prefer is. . ."), you lose them from your pool of future collaborators. A surprising number of people are motivated by a desire to feel needed, to contribute meaningfully, and to share their specific art or skill. When you invite a friend to join you on a project, particularly one on which you lack expertise or on which your friend can share his or her knowledge, both of you will benefit by the enhanced self-esteem that comes in successful collaboration of energy and talent.

Team building and collaboration cannot be a one-way street of manipulation or exploitation. It must be reciprocal. Look for times when your skills and abilities may be of use to the same friends who helped you. Things that come easily and naturally for you may be the very things that your friends find difficult. This is the Christian side of being an opportunist: Search for opportunities to serve others. Until your search for success includes more than personal financial achievements, until you strive to help others succeed as well, you will never find true contentment.

MISTAKE NUMBER SIX

"I CHOOSE **ROMANCE** AND **CHOCOLATE** OVER TRUE LOVE"

Mistake Number Six
"I Choose Romance and Chocolate over True Love"

I love chocolate. As vices and addictions go, it is probably the safest one to have. In fact, several recent medical studies have shown that chocolate is rich in antioxidants and other beneficial nutrients that fight cancer and improve blood circulation. But just as our English language does not distinguish between love for chocolate and true love for another person, we easily confuse romantic infatuation and agapé love.

Scientists have shown that the natural amphetamines in chocolate are remarkably similar to the chemicals the human body generates when one is enamored with a member of the opposite sex. The romantics among us don't wish to believe it, but the euphoric feelings associated with romance are created by biochemical changes in the body more than by some mystical, spiritual phenomenon. Chocolate proves this. If a fine chocolate-covered cherry can bring as much pleasure as a kiss, what does that tell us?

Of course, there are feelings and experiences that love brings us that are deeper than mere chemistry.

Feelings of belonging and purpose that come from meaningful love relationships are reflections of something deeper and more substantial—something that *does* happen at a spiritual level. True love is a profound reality and there is no sin in enjoying its accompanying pleasure, just as it is no sin to bite into a dark Godiva chocolate. The sin is when we don't understand the difference.

Hold this fact foremost in your mind: Romance—infatuation or "puppy love"—is a fleeting pleasure. Because it is rooted in the physical body and our sensory world, by nature it is not going to last. The distinguishing character of true love is that it is eternal.

A man I'll call Jackson came into my office with shocking news. He had decided to leave his wife and children for another woman. He could not yet admit consciously what his subconscious mind had already decided. Like many people who come to the pastor's office in these situations, Jackson was not seeking counsel. He wanted permission and absolution. I was shocked because Jackson was a kind and committed church member; his wife, Eliza, was equally a fine person; and together they seemed like a well-matched, lovely couple. They had been married about ten years and had two cute toddlers. Jackson shared his story: He had met a young, attractive single gal at work, and after spending much time together, they had "fallen in love." The clincher, he confessed, was that whenever Jackson made love with Eliza, he felt like he was cheating on his mistress! This convinced him that this new "love" was the real thing he had been looking for all his life and he should abandon his family and chase after her.

He did not want to hear my advice, but here is what I told him: "Jackson, the key word is *feel*. You *feel* like you are being unfaithful to your mistress by loving your wife, the one with whom you made holy vows, not to mention two children. The *fact* is you made a lifelong love commitment to Eliza, and in turn to your children, and having relations with this coworker has nothing to do with love. It is only about sex. Your feelings are lying to you. If we treat our love relationships like a seafood buffet, moving from one flavor to the next as our appetites drive us, we may end up temporarily satisfied, but in the long run we'll be love hungry and lonely and bereft of any significant family ties." I resisted laying a more direct guilt trip on him about his duty to his children, because my hope was that he would choose the right thing to do in a positive way, rather than being coerced into something against his will that only would have embittered him toward his wife and children. Guilt tends to do that. Another part of me said he deserved a guilt trip, but I wanted what would be best for the children long-term.

My subtle, educational approach did not work, but I doubt a hard-nosed approach would have been any more successful. Most people are slaves to their emotions. Jackson pondered my words and made a short-lived attempt to stick it out with his wife. But shortly thereafter, he left his family and ran off with his mistress. The disruption and pain he caused his ex-wife and abandoned children ruined their lives for several years, though eventually Eliza met a good man and remarried. The children will always carry a scar from their father's desertion. As for Jackson, he later found himself unhappy in his new relationship and chased after another woman, and on and on. I don't know where he is today, but I doubt he is happy. He is one of many examples of "romantic serial monogamists," people whose commitment to their lovers lasts only as long as the high of romance. Then they move on to their next victim—their next monogamous tryst.

Contrast that to what author Ernest Havemann wrote about the romantic love demonstrated in elderly couples:

You can see them alongside the shuffleboard courts in Florida or on the porches of the old folks' homes up North: an old man with snow-white hair, a little hard of hearing, reading the newspaper through a magnifying glass; an old woman in a shapeless dress, her knuckles gnarled by arthritis, wearing sandals to ease her aching arches. They are holding hands, and in a little while they will totter off to take a nap, and then she will cook supper, not a very good supper, and they will watch television, each knowing exactly what the other is thinking, until it is time for bed. They may even have a good, soul-stirring argument, just to prove that they still really care. And through the night they will snore unabashedly, each resting contentedly

because the other is there. They are in love,
they have always been in love, although
sometimes they would have denied it. And
because they have been in love they have
survived everything that life could throw at
them, even their own failures."[1]

If you would like to learn about romance, about
the intimacy of marriage and the power of love, go to a
nursing home and visit patients who are fortunate enough
to still have a living spouse who tends to them. Watch
the faithful, patient love as the healthy spouses tend to
the needs of their bedridden loved ones. It is far more
powerful than any cheap imitation you might see acted
out on television. They daily prove their fulfillment of the
marriage vows, which include the words, "for better, for
worse, for richer, for poorer, in sickness and in health, to
love and to cherish, until we are parted by death."

Dr. Scott Peck also describes this kind of true love:
"Sacrificial love has transforming power. Genuine love
is volitional rather than emotional. The person who truly
loves does so because of a decision to love. This person has
made a commitment to be loving whether or not the loving
feeling is present. If it is, so much the better; but if it isn't,
the commitment to love, the will to love, still stands and is
still exercised. . . . True love is not a feeling by which we
are overwhelmed. It is a committed, thoughtful decision."[2]

I have a suspicion that at many weddings, when the
eloquent words of the apostle Paul in the famous "Love

Chapter" of 1 Corinthians 13 are read, it quickly becomes sentimentalized rather than soberly vowed. The beauty of Paul's words move the heart of the bride and groom, but when they divorce eleven months later, it becomes clear that his words about eternal love were never internalized. Try to look beneath the beauty of Paul's poetry and consider what it might mean for you to live out his teachings on love.

All the great words and deeds of history mean nothing without love. Without love, as Saint Paul says, I am nothing. Of course you remember Charles Dickens's *A Christmas Carol*, and old man Scrooge. He had money and power surrounding a selfish, bitter heart. Finally the "spirits" revealed to Scrooge his own wretched loneliness. They showed him his nothingness in contrast to the humble and loving home of Bob Cratchett and Tiny Tim. The abundant love in the Cratchett home made Scrooge's sacks of gold appear as pennies.

While we're discussing high-class literature, let's take a look at Shakespeare's *King Lear*. Lear was king of England, had a caring family, vast wealth, ultimate power, everything a man could want. But he allowed envy and pettiness to drive him crazy. In the end, responsible for the death of his daughter, with his power dwindling and his royal court in disarray, he confesses, "I am nothing." The one thing he longs for, and lacks, is love. Shakespeare understood 1 Corinthians 13!

A thousand years from now, no one will care if you were famous or rich. No one will care if you were voted employee of the month, no one will care if you had the nicest house in town or how many awards you won or how beautifully you dressed. Your résumé will be dust, your accomplishments in life will be grist for some future archaeologist who finds it amusing that you went to all that trouble for nothing. All you can carry into heaven is your love. Without that, you have nothing. "Everlasting distruction" and being "shut out from the presence of the Lord" is how the Bible describes hell (see 2 Thessalonians 1:9). We are indeed nothing without love.

Another key concept in 1 Corinthians 13 is that love is patient, kind, and steadfast. It bears all things, even bad breath and body odor. Romantic love cannot make that claim. Romantic love is a short-tempered thing, based on outward beauty and comfortable circumstance. Agapé love, Christian love, heroic love, is a different, more powerful thing. Heroic love takes warts and all. This patient love is found in parents when their children disappoint them; among true friends when they find themselves separated by many years and miles; in marriage, when we repeatedly let each other down but never give up.

Here's a humorous story of patience and endurance in marriage. In the 1800s, an elderly woman on the frontier endured the meanness and abuse of her husband for years. One day, the old curmudgeon became ill, fell into a coma, and was believed to be dead. In that place and time, doctors had crude instruments and funeral directors did not practice embalming. So the family dressed the body at home and the pallbearers carried the pine box from the house to the backyard cemetery. As they made their way out of the yard, one pallbearer stumbled, causing the coffin to crash into a gatepost. The jarring impact cracked open the coffin and revived the old mountaineer, who sat up cussing everybody in sight. The man resumed his life with renewed wickedness and for another year abused his wife repeatedly. Finally, he really did die. Once more the body was put in a pine box and the pallbearers carried it from the house. As they shuffled by, the long-suffering widow lifted her head and said in exasperation to the pallbearers, "Please, please, try not to bump the gatepost!"

So love has its limits. Heroic love is not for patsies or wimps. True love is tough love. Heroic love bears all things and hopes all things, but this does not mean that a Christian must act like a milquetoast. True love's unique power helps it withstand the bullies and the abusers of relationships. Though the hero may get weary, he or she never gives up. All things will fade away, but love never ends. Heroic love never shrinks before life's challenges. Heroic love will survive all challengers—even death. Indeed, Paul says, now we see this heroic love in ourselves only dimly. But after we cross over death's threshold, we will see clearly. Love will continue. Love will conquer. Love is the embodiment of all that is good, all that is lasting, the very essence of divinity. Love is the greatest of all things, not because it feels good, but because it does good. Love does make the world go round. Love is the glue that holds us together as people. Love is the hand that holds us steady and lifts us up from despair into hope.

As a pastor, watching tender romantics jump (or be tossed) from one relationship to another frustrates and pains me. The romantics hold fast to the illusion that they are on a search for perfect love. If only I could get them to see in the mirror more objectively: Their weak, cowardly love and serial monogamy lacks nobility. It is really just an obsessive grasping for pleasure.

We are created by a God of love for the purpose of loving. In Genesis, it says that God made humanity in His own image. If God's nature and character is one of love and we are made in God's image, then we, too, have a natural tendency to want love. We are born to love. However, sin has distorted our natural desire to give and receive love. If we will fulfill our natural longing to love God, the benefits are real. We find purpose in living. We fill the void in our soul. We begin to experience God's love in a better way.

May our battle with Narcissus end with these words from 1 John 4:11–12: "Since God so loved us, we also ought to love one another. No one has ever seen God; but if we love one other, God lives in us and his love is made complete in us."

Love is all we need—not some cheap imposter of love, not infatuation or fondness, but a deep, self-sacrificial, committed love for God and for one another. All you need is love.

~~~

Notes

1. *Bits & Pieces*, June 24, 1993, 7–9.

2. Ibid.

SOLUTION NUMBER SIX

"I CAN LEARN TO **TAME** MY MIND AND EMOTIONS"

Solution Number Six
"I Can Learn to Tame My Mind and Emotions"

Your brain indeed has a "mind of its own." The proof of this is that we dream. Sometimes my dreams are completely foreign to my waking life. And I certainly do not initiate nightmares; they come without invitation. Secular thinkers tend to identify "self" with "mind," but in the Judeo-Christian framework, the spirit/soul/self is superior to the tangle of neurons and electrochemical processes inside the human skull. And scripture clearly teaches that we can harness and control our mental processes by the application of self-will. We *can* choose our thoughts.

Two giant obstacles can interfere with our freedom of choice and thought: self-deception and addiction. The two are connected. We continue to lie to ourselves and try to believe that pleasure equals contentment. I hope you have heard loud and clear that I do not think pleasure is evil. But when we assume that pleasure is the *ultimate good*, the essential aim and end in life, we set out on a journey to nowhere. American society, as a whole, is on that journey, and the proof is reflected in the prevalence of drug abuse and addiction.

Addiction, the obsessive and uncontrollable urge
to repeatedly engage in an action, presents the clearest
example of the fallacy of seeking contentment through
objects of pleasure. While addiction is more complex
than simply a craving for pleasure, the pleasure centers
of the brain do reinforce the cycle of addiction. Addiction
is caused partly by a desire to escape pain, and because
pleasure is usually thought of as the opposite of pain,
pleasure seems to be the solution. Of course, what we see
in addicts is that the blind pursuit of pleasure becomes the
problem, and the original problem is forgotten (though
still present). My thesis is that pleasure can only mask the
misery, not cure it. The opposite of pain—*contentment*—
cannot be pursued directly but comes as a consequence of
facing up to our problems.

An action becomes addicting partly because it is
never fully satisfying. This should be obvious. If an action
were fully satisfying, we would not need to "go back to
the well" repeatedly to be quenched. Common addictions,
such as alcohol and other drugs, sex addictions, eating
disorders—and even what I call "mall-itis," the addiction
to shopping—attract people like a mirage; they create the
illusion of satisfaction because they make us feel very good
at the moment. But just like mirages, addiction illusions
are in our minds, not in reality. Whether an addictive behavior triggers the pleasure-giving endorphins in the brain
or merely satisfies a psychological craving, the behavior
does not change reality. Moreover, because in addiction we
have ignored the cry of our souls in favor of the cry of our

bodies and minds, we still have a deep thirst that propels us back time and time again to our addictive behavior. The scientific explanation of addiction is more complex than we tackle here, but it is not unscientific to say, in lay terms, that addiction is the adoption of a lie, either in the body, the mind, or both. The human body does not normally need heroin for survival; instead, the heroin-addicted body accepts a false reality that to survive it must have heroin. The adopted lie becomes the new reality for the addict; the addiction takes on a life of its own, and the addict's craving, which at one point was merely a passing thought, becomes externalized into reality.

We might describe addiction as a "drive externalizing as modes of obsessive need-fulfillment." The acronym for this is DEMON, and as corny and contrived as that might seem, the concept of a demon can be a helpful metaphor. Psychiatrist Scott Peck and theologian/psychologist George Hunter both have hinted that they believe demons are real entities that can inhabit and plague humans. However, it is not necessary to believe in the supernatural to find the concept of demonic power a useful one. In the Bible, we find these traits of demons:

1. They are distinct, separate creatures that can inhabit human beings.

2. They have a distinct personality, which is evil.

3. They tell lies.

4. They impair the functioning of their host.

5. They are extremely hard to expel.

Addictions are demonic in the sense that they develop a personality of their own, they deceive their host, they impair their host's ability to function, and they are not easily cured. When addictions are seen in this light, we tend to take them more seriously as the great adversarial threat that they are. Modern terminology tends to refer to addiction as a disease, which it is. But it is more than a bad cold. Addiction is demonic in the sense that demons will actively fight the physician, will viciously resist the healing process even if it causes the destruction of the host and his or her family and friends. This should make us cautious when dealing with severe addictions.

More has been written about alcoholism than about any other addiction; therefore, it would be profitable to look at the treatment of alcoholism if we wish to learn about the treatment of addictions in general. The Alcoholics Anonymous organization has the best success rate of any addiction program (when you consider that they are not selective about who they treat). Part of the success of AA in fighting addiction is that they deal with one of the root causes: deception or lies. The first thing AA requires of its members is a confession, an honest statement of their predicament: "Hello, my name is Bill, and I'm an alcoholic." This is the essential step in recovery from any addiction: breaking loose from the circles of self-deception in which the addict has been enslaved. Usually this affirmation of the truth (that I'm addicted and need help) does not come solely from the addict. It requires another person's intervention (family, friend, or the legal system) to convince the addict of his or her problem. Addicts then depend on other people (most effectively, other reformed addicts) for the duration of their recovery.

The second important aspect of AA is that they admit the problem is bigger than any human can handle. They call upon a higher power to help them.

And of course, they commit themselves to abstinence. They don't worry about next year, just about today, with the belief that anyone, with God's help, can stay sober twenty-four hours.

A final step in the AA program is to seek the forgiveness of those the addict has harmed, partly in order that the addict might forgive himself (or herself) and be forgiven.

These steps (AA has twelve in all, but these are the most important for our discussion here) correspond to the actions that Jesus took in dealing with demon possession. He would "name" the demon, thereby identifying the problem but also confronting the demon and in effect saying, "Aha, I know you're there." Second, Jesus said that exorcism required the invocation of a higher power (God) through prayer. Third, abstinence (fasting) was required. And in most healing miracles performed by Christ, He would say, "Your sins are forgiven." These are also the steps necessary to free us from addictions (see

Mark 9:14–29). And without freedom, we can never find
contentment.

Even those of us who are not addicted in some
form or another can learn from the causes and cures for
addictive behavior. Addictive behavior is the extreme
consequence of believing demonic lies about pleasure.
What lies do you believe about yourself and your world?

The Christian worldview recognizes the powerful
reality of active evil. As C. S. Lewis put it, every inch of
the universe is claimed by God and counterclaimed by
the devil. In other words, we are soldiers in the midst
of a territorial war between good and evil. In warfare,
if your enemy has bigger numbers and better weapons,
what would you do? Storming them in a head-on assault
would be suicidal. Instead, the wise warrior would opt
for a sneak attack. Guerilla warfare works in our battles
against that giant adversary, addiction. Don't battle
obsessions, addictions, or naggingly negative thoughts
head-on. Sneak up on them. The more you contemplate
and fret over a negative compulsion, the larger it looms in
your mind and the more stressed you become. Ironically,
you will find yourself turning to that very obsession for
comfort in the face of your stress. Exceptions prove the
rule. For every story of an alcoholic who successfully
won his battle over the bottle by engaging in a daily
staring contest with a full liquor glass, there are hundreds
of others who learned they must not have alcohol in
their homes or on their minds. When you catch yourself
dwelling on a hauntingly negative thought or temptation,

the best course of action is to change the subject!

AA and other professional rehab organizations, along with Christian counselors, psychologists, and psychiatrists, are the front line in the battle against addiction. But another key for addicts who want to be set free is to improve their overall health. Addicts tend to be unhealthy in a variety of ways that may not be a result of their addiction. In fact, sometimes poor health drives the addiction. The most common example is a person who is overweight and begins to have back pain. To ease the pain, he begins to take a prescription drug. A few months later, he finds himself addicted to the narcotic pain medication. I cannot prove it statistically, but by personal observation and anecdotal evidence, I am convinced that a great deal of addiction stems from people who have failed to take care of their overall health.

In my high school days, dissecting frogs was an unpleasant but interesting part of biology class. To learn about the human body, doctors and scientists have dissected it (literally and figuratively) and have pondered the minutiae of the human mind and body. Such a piecemeal approach is fine for scientists, but it is not a particularly helpful way for us to seek good health. Though "holistic health" is a buzz phrase sometimes abused by medical quacks, it is indeed best to look at ourselves holistically.

In ancient times, as reflected in the Bible, the Jewish understanding of the human creature was holistic. The interconnectedness of mind, body, and spirit is taught throughout the Old Testament. One source of confusion is that we tend to mistranslate the biblical/Hebrew word for *soul* as an "invisible spirit," when actually it referred to the body—but even then, the word *soul* meant more than just the physical flesh. It connoted the entire being. The Hebrews taught that a human soul is a combination of heart and mind, spirit and body. Deuteronomy 6:5 tells us to "love the LORD your God with all your heart and with all your soul." They used the word *heart* to speak more of the intangible parts of human personality, such as emotions and volition, whereas they used *soul* to refer to the physical body as well as the spirit. In any case, these terms overlap.

Anyone seeking the good life of health and happiness would do well to heed the Hebrew scriptures and nurture all aspects of one's spiritual, physical, moral, and emotional health.

In recent years, we have all learned how a good mental attitude helps sustain good physical health. Doctors warn us that stress and negative thinking can cause more than ulcers. Heart disease, gastrointestinal disorders, and even some forms of cancer have been shown in clinical studies and by anecdotal evidence to be more common and more chronic in negative, depressed personalities than in people who are upbeat and easygoing. However, knowledge is not enough. We need to act on that fact!

How can we enhance our mental health? Some proven principles and mental disciplines are just as important to our overall health as diet and exercise.

Start by making a decision to change your

thoughts. Yes, some thoughts are beyond our control. Dark clouds and pessimism may be part of a person's natural way of looking at the world. If your mind seems to go automatically toward a negative mode, you may have to work very hard to consciously take control of your thoughts. We might not control what pops into our minds, but we can control what lingers there. As Martin Luther put it, "We cannot stop birds from flying overhead, but we can keep them from building nests in our hair."

The quickest way to begin is to change what I call your *predominant mental fixation*. For too many of us, our predominant mental fixation is television. TV can be a fun, relaxing break for the mind for an hour or so a day. But when it is our *central* pursuit, we rob our physical health by becoming inactive coach potatoes, and we starve our minds and spirits of healthier fare. Vary your mental routine. When your favorite show ends, don't channel surf to find some meager replacement. Turn off the set, turn on a lamp, and read a book. During the summer months, when it stays daylight longer, go outside, take a nature walk or a boat ride. Pondering God's beautiful creation is like eating a lean steak with a salad: It is both satisfying and strengthening. On cold or rainy days, vary your mental "diet" with music.

Often when I've shared with others the fact that I play guitar, someone will say, "Oh, I used to play guitar. . .but I don't get around to it much anymore." I can't imagine letting musical talent lie dormant. If you know how to play an instrument—wonderful! Dust off your keyboard, guitar, or flute and make some music. If you cannot play an instrument, you could at least bang on some bongos or a chord organ. Even passive listening to music can be more stimulating to the brain than television. The Bible records that when King Saul was suffering from mental disturbances, depression, and anxiety, the music of David's harp soothed him greatly. Music is the single best medicine for a stressed-out mind.

Yet another way to feed your mind is by intellectual interaction with others. Join a talk salon, study group, or book club. Or play chess, bridge, or Scrabble, games that require mental exertion and focus while still providing fun and relaxation. In my office are two very durable houseplants. They have survived my hit-and-miss watering and my nearly total neglect in feeding them, but they usually look pathetic. When I finally remembered to give the plants some fertilizer, they perked up with beautiful, new green leaves. If an organism as simple as a plant needs fertilizer, how much more does the complex human brain need to be nourished? Find tangible ways to nourish your mind. Filling your mind with positive thoughts is easier said than done. It requires more than just the decision to change your thinking; we must implement some pragmatic methods for mental rejuvenation. Think. Decide. Then *act*!

Positive thinking is a decision that creates a positive environment. Even when things around us are not positive, we can still find a refuge of hope in a peaceful mind and spirit. But we must make a conscious effort to build that refuge and to return to it daily. The apostle Paul said, "Whatever is true, whatever is honorable, whatever is just, whatever is pure, whatever is pleasing, whatever is commendable. . .think about these things" (Philippians 4:8 NRSV).

If you haven't read about the power of positive thinking, by famous authors Norman Vincent Peale or Napoleon Hill, you may benefit by further description of the concept. The principle of positive thinking was summed up by Hill in the slogan, "Whatever the mind can conceive and believe, it can achieve." Positive thinking is a mind-set that can transform your life and improve your health. Positive thinkers expect good things to happen: If they trip and fall into a mud puddle, they get up and feel in their pockets for fish! Jesus was just such a person! His disciples looked into a little boy's lunch basket and saw a few meager pieces of fish and bread; Jesus looked in the same basket and saw a feast for five thousand!

Of course, Jesus had more going for Him than mere positive thinking. He reminded us that the spiritual version of mental optimism is *faith*! He said that even a tiny speck of faith can move mountains. The secular principle of positive thinking is only a shadow of the more powerful Christian application of faith—but I do believe a first step for non-Christians is to be proactive in commanding one's thinking and attitude.

Successful people believe in themselves despite any negativity around them. Consider the U.S. presidents of the last fifty years. If we look at things negatively, it was *impossible* for any of them to have been elected! Truman couldn't be president; he didn't have a college education. Eisenhower couldn't be president; he had a heart condition. Kennedy couldn't be president; he wore a back brace and had several chronic illnesses. Nixon couldn't be president; he had already tried and failed against Kennedy. Ronald Reagan was too old to be president, and Bill Clinton was too young. And, according to the critics, the elder George Bush had no charisma, and the younger Bush had no brains (but he was smart enough not to believe his detractors). Regardless of their politics, these men had at least two things in common: They all believed they *could* become president—and they did!

What do you believe you can become? What is your mind telling your body? Is your lack of planning for the future subtly telling your subconscious mind that your future is bleak?

The wisdom of the ancients tells us that positive thinking is essential to health and happiness. Marcus Aurelius wrote, "A man's life is what his thoughts make it." King Solomon said, "As a man thinks in his heart, so is he." Ralph Waldo Emerson opined, "A man is what he thinks about all day long." Paul of Tarsus, a great proponent of the power of positive thinking, penned the famous words: "Be transformed by the renewing of your minds."

The principle of positive thinking, of never-ending hope in the face of adversity, is found throughout Jesus' life and teachings. In a dark time in history, He was a man who had a clear purpose, a positive attitude, and unswerving confidence. In all He did, Christ demonstrated that faith—the religious equivalent of positive thinking—can surmount any obstacle. He said, "If you have faith as small as a mustard seed, you can say to this mountain, 'Move from here to there' and it will move" (Matthew 17:20).

For Jesus, faith is not so much a thought as it is an action. The story of Jesus walking on the water is a powerful demonstration of this fact. In that one faith action, Jesus proved that the impossible is possible. The negative naysayer could not see it. I'd bet some pessimistic, cynical spectator on the shore said, "Look at that Jesus guy—He can't even swim!"

We all know negative people in our lives who tell us that our plans and dreams are impossible. Do you let those discouraging people dissuade you from taking action? Do the nabobs of negativity convince you to think small, to give up on the miraculous?

We must broaden our vision. Don't be like the little boy in this joke: Kenny's teacher asked the class to count the number of stars they could see at night. Answers reported the next day were varied, from hundreds to thousands. But little Kenny answered, "I only counted six." The puzzled teacher asked, "How is it that you saw so few stars when the other children found so many?" Kenny replied, "Well, our backyard is awfully small."

How big is your yard? How big is your imagination? How broad is your vision? How strong is your belief in the good possibilities of life? Taming your mind, your attitude, and your point of view and perspective can make all the difference between success and failure, health and illness. A little bit of faith can lead to great action and, ultimately, to something miraculous.

MISTAKE NUMBER SEVEN

"I'M TOO BUSY BEING REACTIVE TO BE PROACTIVE"

Mistake Number Seven
"I'm Too Busy Being Reactive to Be Proactive"

Serena is anything but serene. She describes herself as the steel ball in a pinball machine, bouncing from one bumper to another, thrown to and fro continuously by forces beyond her control. Or so she thinks. Serena tends to blame the world for her erratic motion through life. But unlike a pinball, she is not an inert object. She could choose to redirect her life. And most of the force that pushes her into wild actions and mood swings are actually not from the bumps in life but are driven by her overreaction to troubles. Everybody faces problems. But reactionary people turn molehills into mountains, recoil in fear at minor setbacks, and create whole new sets of problems for themselves by their overreactions.

Serena often falls victim to the N-types of the world. Gabe, a particularly obnoxious N-type, made an ugly remark about Serena at a party. For Gabe, it was an attempt at humor at Serena's expense. Her low self-esteem made her an easy target, and it did not matter to Gabe that his comment was completely untrue. With one exception, everyone at the party viewed Gabe as an idiot, and at the moment of his insult, they all thought even less

of him and felt good feelings for Serena. But Serena was
the one exception. Rather than realizing that Gabe's insult
had backfired, Serena was embarrassed and exploded
with rage. With tears rolling down her face, she screamed,
"That's not true! You are an absolute jerk!" and ran out
of the room. Suddenly her emotional overreaction made
her the object of whispered concern. Most people had
learned to dismiss Gabe's silly remarks and childish, petty
sense of humor. Objectively, Serena's anger was certainly
understandable. But her public loss of control made
everyone uncomfortable and in a perverse way made Gabe
appear for a moment as the aggrieved one and Serena as
a bit rash and unreasonable. To make matters worse, the
next time Serena received an invitation to a party, she
stayed home because she feared Gabe would be there. This
only increased the talk behind her back that she was an
unstable person. Being reactive creates problems greater
than the initial trigger.

The proof of this is found in observing nonreactive
people. Some folks just coast through life relaxed and
unflappable. In observing laid-back, carefree souls, we
can learn to emulate them and take things in stride. Keep
an image in your mind of a carefree, confident, calm
friend. When trouble brews, try to picture how he or she
would react (or *not* react). Try this exercise—you may be
surprised how easy it is to adopt a better habit of response
to stress simply by picturing a calm and cool persona. If
you have no carefree friends, think of how a character
such as Groucho Marx, Hawkeye Pierce, or Bugs Bunny

would deal with the "crisis" you are facing!

You may still find it difficult not to be reactive. It may even feel like we're not standing up for ourselves if we cease being reactive. That is probably not the case, however. Review your life and play "connect the dots." I'd bet you would find many of the more difficult and unpleasant things that have happened in your life stem from having overreacted to situations.

I do not want this book to portray neuroses as something to be proud of. I do not wish to convey the impression that being neurotic is an excuse that somehow justifies all kinds of misbehavior. Comedian Flip Wilson used to say, "I can't help myself. . .the devil made me do it." Neurosis does not *make* us do anything, and it is a cop-out to resign ourselves to a reactive, self-centered, whining lifestyle.

The hard truth is that neurosis is itself evil. As painful as neurosis is, the syndrome emerged as an unhealthy coping mechanism designed (subconsciously) to soften or avoid pain and suffering in our lives—usually, pain that comes from our critics. Psychologist Carl G. Jung asserted, "Neurosis is always a substitute for legiti-mate suffering." I have finally realized that I gain a sick pleasure in nursing my self-pity and that my neurosis can indeed be a substitute problem that I use to keep my real problems at a distance. Dr. Thomas Lane Butts adds:

"In time, the substitute becomes more painful than the legitimate suffering it

was designed to avoid. Then we substitute
a substitute for the substitute and build
layer after layer of neurotic responses until
we lose touch with the problem originally
avoided. People I see as a counselor often
come in wanting help with their most recent
substitute. More often than not, it becomes
obvious that it is not about what they think
it is about; it is about something else. And
we never know what it is really about until
the layers of substitutes are peeled away
and we get to the original problem that was
too painful to solve."[1]

Discovering and identifying your underlying
problems can be difficult. It may require years of
psychotherapy. Nevertheless, you can find immediate
symptomatic relief by following the pragmatic suggestions
in this book. The most important of these is to cease being
reactive. Instead, be proactive and lead with advance
planning rather than after-the-fact damage control.

Being proactive requires creativity. If you can
invent a solution to a problem even before the problem is
fully formed, life becomes much easier. My theory is that
neurotics tend to be creative people. Jung implied as much
in his statement that neurotics have created an illusory
pain in order to mask their real pain. Let us instead
turn our tendency upside down: Rather than using our
creativity to weave elaborate escapist fantasies, let's use

our inventiveness to come up with fun and novel ways of coping with problems in proactive ways.

Unfortunately, if you were not born with a creative gene, few colleges can teach it. You may take a course in creative writing, but the professors often assume that you are already creative! In the next chapter, we will consider some simple, practical exercises to increase your creativity and proactivity, as well as some tips for honing your goal-setting skills.

~~~

Notes:

1. From a personal letter to the author from Dr. Thomas Lane Butts.

SOLUTION NUMBER SEVEN

"I WILL TURN **DREAMS** INTO GOALS INTO **REALITY**"

Solution Number Seven
"I Will Turn Dreams into Goals into Reality"

As a child, my favorite way of getting out of trouble
when I did something wrong was to say, "I didn't do it
on purpose." Even to this day, when my wife gets upset
about something I've done, I catch myself saying, "Well, I
didn't do it on purpose." Sadly, this may apply in a broader
way to the lives of many people. There are many who go
through life aimlessly, live only for themselves, never have
any purpose or direction or integrity, and when they die, the
most appropriate epitaph for their tombstone would be "I
didn't do it on purpose." Which is another way of saying,
as the writer of Ecclesiastes also said, "All is vanity."

What a terrible tragedy to live your life without
purpose. I'm sure you've all heard of Alfred Nobel, famous
for establishing the Nobel Prizes for peace, medicine,
physics, etc. Nobel first became famous and successful as
a chemist. He invented a useful product called dynamite,
which he envisioned as an aid to construction and
mining—which it was. But he was horrified to see it also
used extensively in warfare.

One day he picked up the newspaper and was
shocked to read his own obituary. It seems that a relative

with the same name had died, and the press had confused
him with the famous Alfred Nobel. The obituary mentioned
the usual things about Nobel's life, giving him credit
for the invention of dynamite—which, it said, was used
in bombs. Nothing much good was printed, which made
Nobel realize that, for all his work and wealth, he had
done almost nothing worthwhile. Consequently, he decided
to use his wealth to set up a trust fund and created a
perpetual committee to ensure that great achievements
throughout history would be marked by the Nobel Prize.

What will *your* obituary say? How will you be
remembered? What is your purpose in being here? Are
you making any significant improvement in the lives of
those around you? The measure of success is not in fame
or wealth—and that's true also for someone like Alfred
Nobel. It wasn't that he wanted to be rich or famous—he
already was through the invention of dynamite—but he
wanted to give something back to the world. On our own
scale, you and I can do likewise.

Unfortunately, most people never discover their
purpose in life. They have no direction, no goals, no
meaningful reason for living. They may have fantasies
and pipe dreams. But they have never made any concrete
decision about their future. They have never found a
purpose in living or a plan for tomorrow.

Psychologist William Moulton asked three
thousand people, "What do you live for?" He found that
94 percent were simply enduring the present, hoping for
something better in the future. Other surveys have shown

that most people never have definable goals in life.

Here's the bottom line: We can begin today to make something of ourselves, or we can simply stumble blindly through life without purpose, drifting aimlessly from place to place, from job to job, from relationship to relationship.

The question is not, "What are you going to do for a living?" but "What are you going to do *with* your living?" Your purpose, my purpose, our purpose, is to love and serve one another.

The world is going to tell you to look out for number one. Go for the gusto. Get all you can for yourself. But if you listen to the world, you will have no purpose. You will sink in a pool of despair and meaninglessness. And at the end of your life, you may feel like Woody Allen, who said, "My only regret in life is that I wasn't somebody else."

Anthony Campolo surveyed a large group of ninety-five-year-olds, asking them, "If you could live your life over, what would you do differently?" The most common response was: "I would do things that would last beyond my lifetime."

If you listen to Jesus, He will ask you to follow Him to a higher purpose—and a higher happiness. You can make up your mind now to serve God. By lending a helping hand to others. By living righteously. By giving of your time, talents, and treasure. God has a plan and purpose for you. Find it.

Ponder this rhyme by an anonymous poet:

There was a very cautious man
Who never laughed or played.
He never gave, he never tried,
He never sang or prayed!
And when one day he passed away
His insurance was denied
For since he never really lived,
They claimed he never died!

I hope you decide to live a full life, to follow God's plan. And I pray that at the end of your days in this world, you can say happily about your life, "I did it on purpose."

The Purpose-Driven Life by Rick Warren is a runaway best-seller filled with good advice, but Warren would be the first to admit that others have previously emphasized the importance of purpose and goals. In a previous chapter, I mentioned the name Napoleon Hill. Hill spent years interviewing the five hundred wealthiest men in America for a book titled *Think and Grow Rich*. The key to success, he said, was *goal setting*, having a plan. He also listed thirty-one major causes of failure, and the number one cause was *lack of a well-defined purpose in life*. Hill writes: "There is no hope of success for the person who does not have a central purpose, or definite goal at which to aim."

What is true about business success is also true of life in general. Long before Rick Warren or Napoleon Hill was born, the apostle Paul emphasized the importance of goal setting. In Ephesians, Paul lays out exactly what our purpose should be: Christian maturity. He uses the Greek word *teleios*, which means "a finished product, the complete and perfect human, a fullness of integrity and virtue, maturity." This maturation process is what John Wesley called "sanctification," the growth toward spiritual holiness and perfection in love. The New Testament letter to the Ephesians is a detailed blueprint, a plan we should follow in the journey to maturity. Let's move through Paul's blueprint point by point. To aid your memory, each of Paul's points in this epistle begins with the letter *s*:

1. *Study*. Study the plan. Study the scriptures. The third chapter of Ephesians encourages us to learn the plan of God. Paul said he wants "to make everyone see what is the plan of. . .God who created all things" (Ephesians 3:9 NRSV).

There are three ways to build a house: without plans, with your own plans, and with plans drawn up by an architect.

My grandmother had a house built without plans. It was a disaster. The front doorframe was built like a trapezoid, one side taller than the other, so they just tacked a triangular strip of wood onto the top of the door to fill the gap. When you build without a plan, you have to do a lot of patchwork!

A second and better way to build a house is to

draw up your own plans. I built my garage that way, and it came out surprisingly well. The plans, even though I drew them up myself, made for more efficient use of materials and yielded a very serviceable building. But it still looks like an amateur designed it. We can recognize houses that were built from plans drawn up by amateurs. They're square and neat but often have poorly designed traffic flow, wasted space, and boring aesthetics.

So the third and best way to build a house is to use the plans of a master architect; plans designed by someone with great experience and ability, someone who can present to you a near-perfect model of what the end product should look like. This is what the apostle Paul teaches: Use the plan of God, the master architect of life! Paul speaks of God "who created all things" and who has an "eternal purpose." That purpose, that master plan, is recorded in the Bible. Of course, no matter how good your blueprints are, if you fail to study the design, you'll end up with a house that looks like my grandmother's. So study the Word, and build your life upon it.

2. *Serve*. Serve Christ. Serve the church. Again, Paul teaches this in Ephesians. When he speaks of building up the church, he is not referring to a church building but to the body of believers, brothers and sisters in Christ. When new members join the church, they are asked to take a vow of service: "Will you

uphold the church by your prayers, your
presence, your gifts, and your service?"

Ephesians 4:12–13 explains that maturity comes
through service. The Lord "prepare[s] God's people for
works of service, so that the body of Christ may be built up
until we all reach unity in the faith and in the knowledge of
the Son of God and become mature, attaining to the whole
measure of the fullness of Christ."

Although studying the Bible is essential to the
Christian life, in my experience the most mature Christians
are not the Bible scholars. The most mature Christians are
those who have given their lives in service to others.

3. *Speak the truth.* Ephesians 4:15–16 says,
"Speaking the truth in love, we will in
all things grow up into him who is the
Head, that is, Christ. From him the whole
body, joined and held together by every
supporting ligament, grows and builds
itself up in love, as each part does its
work."

Everyone would agree that a mature person is an
honest person. But did you ever consider that the very act
of speaking the truth helps you grow and mature? This
includes facing the truth about yourself. At times, it may be
painful to see truthfully how imperfect we are, how much
room there is for improvement and growth. At other times,

we hide from our true potential, who we truly can be.

Consider the old Native American tale about an eagle's egg that rolled down the mountain and landed in the nest of a prairie chicken. The eaglet hatched with the brood of chicks and never knew the truth—that he was an eagle, not a chicken. He clucked and cackled and scratched the dirt for insects to eat, just like his adopted siblings. Years passed, but even as an adult eagle, he still lived with the chickens, never flying more than a few feet, settling for life in the dust. One day he saw a magnificent bird flying far above. With graceful majesty on the wind, it soared to wonderful heights on its golden wings. "What a beautiful bird," said the ignorant prairie eagle. "What is it?" A friend clucked back, "That's an eagle, the chief of birds. But don't give it a second thought. We could never fly like that." So the eagle went back to pecking at grubs and died having accepted the lie that he was nothing but a chicken.

Truth is a very powerful agent of change and growth. Discover the truth, and you'll soar to new spiritual heights!

    4. *Share.* We spoke of this earlier, but it bears repeating. Generosity is essential to spiritual growth. Ephesians 4:28 states, "Thieves must give up stealing; rather let them labor and work honestly with their own hands, so as to have something to share with the needy" (NRSV). The Bible

teaches that the purpose of work is not
to get rich but to be able to share! Until
you accept that truth, you'll never be a
mature Christian.

God's plan is for sharing. It's the first thing one
learns in kindergarten. But some adults forget that lesson
and become spoiled children again, in effect saying, "This
is mine; you can't have it." Generosity is the mark of
maturity.

5. *Submit to one another, submit to Christ.*
   Alongside generosity is the associated
   principle of submission—another form of
   sharing. Ephesians 5:21 says, "Submit to
   one another out of reverence for Christ."
   Just as we should share our material
   wealth, we also are to share power.
   That's what submission means. Christians
   don't abuse whatever authority or status
   or position we may hold, whether in
   the church, on the job, or in the home.
   Mature people don't cling to or fight over
   power. They share power and empower
   others. Submission and humility are
   signs of strength, not weakness. People of
   strong character and mature spirit want
   to see others develop their talents. They
   do not squash them with power.

Sharing power helps us mature. When we humble ourselves, we are more receptive to criticism. I learn and grow only when people are comfortable in telling me where I need growth. So make maturity your goal. Maturity is not just "growing up." Maturity is not just learning great axioms. Maturity comes by learning about yourself and having the self-discipline to change in light of that self-knowledge. No universal axiom will replace self-knowledge and self-discipline, the building blocks of maturity. Not even Paul's advice will make us mature until we make the effort at self-discipline.

Follow Paul's blueprint. Understand the "S-plan," or as Ephesians 5:17 puts it, "Understand what the Lord's will is." Then set clear goals to achieve your purpose in life. However, we must go beyond mere knowledge and goal setting. We must reach for the goal, strive for the prize. I conclude with these words from Paul: "Forgetting what is behind and straining toward what is ahead, I press on toward the goal to win the prize for which God has called me heavenward in Christ Jesus" (Philippians 3:13–14).

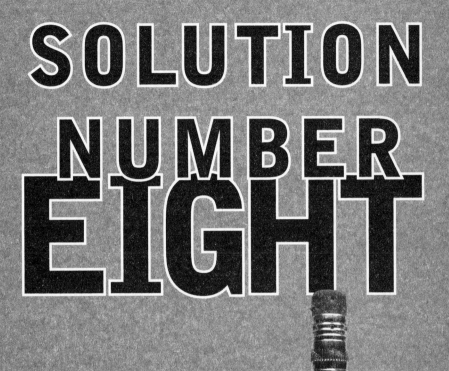

SOLUTION NUMBER EIGHT

"I WILL **LIVE** **BEYOND** MYSELF"

Solution Number Eight
"I Will Live beyond Myself"

If you live on planet Earth, you have been hurt. Rejected by a lover, criticized too harshly by a parent, harassed by a boss, ridiculed by a group. In most cases, I don't think our neurosis was caused by that hurt; we were probably born with a tender nervous system and fragile emotions. But whatever the cause, highly sensitive people certainly are more harshly affected by life's rejections. We are walking wounded. We carry our pain with us. Most of us have been carrying it since childhood—a shiny, accumulated collection. I'm still carrying pain from my toddler years, as I explained in an earlier chapter, when I told the kitty in my lap, "You are the only one who loves me."

I lied to the cat. I almost believed the lie. The lie of self-pity nursed me in some perverted, unhealthy, satisfying way. Maybe that is okay for a four-year-old, but the message my grown-up self needs to hear is, "Get over it!"

Severe trauma naturally shifts people into a self-protective survival mode. Neurotics tend to stay in that mode even without a great trauma. We curl up into a ball of nursing self-absorption. That narcissistic state only exacerbates our condition, cutting us off from meaningful relationships, keeping us from engaging the best joys and achievements of life. The unhealthy condition of codependency, in which we spend most of our energies trying to fix the crazy people around us, is actually another manifestation of self-centeredness. Codependents are driven to take care of others in order to mask our own pain. The life Christ calls us to is not sniveling, groveling codependency. The only cure, the only path to the life God intends for us, is to *genuinely* move beyond ourselves by conscious choice and pure motive. Break out of that narcissistic shell and live in the big, wide world!

We have several clichés or labels for outstanding individuals who live "the good life." We say they are "bigger than life," "living large," or "a big person." To live beyond ourselves means to expand our horizons, to engage as much of the human community as possible. Be a big person. Make a difference in the world. Aim to have something bigger inscribed on your tombstone than the tiny epitaph, "Sadder than the fact he died is the fact he never tried."

The paradox is that adopting such a "larger than life" persona begins with humility—a surrender of self and a death of ego. Jesus said, "For whoever wants to save his life will lose it, but whoever loses his life for me and for the gospel will save it" (Mark 8:35). Christian charity is not only something we do for others, it is also beneficial for us. The more of ourselves we give away (our time, talents, thoughts, treasures), the more we connect with the broader world and the more fulfilled we become. But our *motivation* must be pure and selfless. To lead the large life beyond myself must be a choice made out of humility, love, and a willingness to reach out in ways that are not first and foremost self-serving.

One of my mentors, Dr. James Fowler, author and director of the Center for Faith Development at Emory University, has spent a lifetime dealing with questions such as, What are the stages of faith? What can we do to grow in faith and self-actualization? What constitutes spiritual maturity? He asserts that the final stage of faith, the mark of maturity, comes when a person begins caring for others and actively teaching the next generation. Give yourself to others. Pass the torch. Pay it forward.

We are all teachers of sorts. We are teaching those who observe our lives. We may never know how we affect the world, for good or ill. We never know how a simple action today could possibly affect the whole world tomorrow. We never know who is watching our virtues and vices.

Dr. Kevin Lagree lives large. He has made a difference in the world. The former dean of Emory University's Candler School of Theology has said that he would never have become a lawyer, teacher, and dean if not for the example set by some faithful Christians in his past. He did not become a Christian as a young boy. His parents never took him to church. He never learned about God's love. He never experienced Christian fellowship. Until one day, at about age twelve, he read *To*

Kill a Mockingbird. If you've read the book, you know that the hero of the story is a Christian lawyer named Atticus Finch, a fictional example of someone who lives beyond himself. Young Kevin was so impressed by the virtuous character of Atticus Finch that he decided to become a lawyer himself.

One day a real lawyer came to Kevin's school to give a talk. After the class, Kevin went up to speak to him. The lawyer immediately saw something special in young Kevin. And he did a strange thing: He didn't invite Kevin to visit his law office—he invited Kevin Lagree to visit his *church.* Kevin did, and for the first time discovered the joy of Christian fellowship.

So whatever Dr. Kevin Lagree accomplishes in service to God is a result of the example of a *fictional* lawyer and a simple invitation from a *real* lawyer to attend church. How many times have we failed to make the tiny effort to invite someone to our church? Might we have brought someone like Kevin Lagree to Christ?

That lawyer may never have known that by his simple kindness he inspired a child, who became dean of a seminary that trains thousands of pastors, who in turn will lead ten thousand churches, which affect millions of people in a billion positive ways!

But some of you may still say, "Hey, I'm just a nobody from a little old town in the middle of nowhere. What can I do?" Guess what? It was a "nobody" from the small town of Monroeville, Alabama, where I once lived, who wrote *To Kill a Mockingbird.* My friend Harper

Lee never dreamed she would change the lives of millions of readers who have read her now-classic tale. It was a "nobody" from the tiny hamlet of Magnolia Springs, just a stone's throw from where I now live, who wrote *Forrest Gump*. Winston Groom had no idea his book would be made into an Academy Award–winning movie and touch the lives of millions with a positive message of love.

"But," you might say, "I'm not a Harper Lee or Winston Groom. I'm a nobody from a little old town, but I ain't never writ a book." Well, then, I'll tell you of another "nobody" from a little town in Georgia. She faithfully taught a Sunday school class in a tiny Baptist church. She felt like this was a good thing to do, and she really cared about her handful of young students. But she didn't know that one of the little boys she was teaching would grow up to be president of the United States. Jimmy Carter credits that Sunday school teacher with much of his success and character. The values of love and peace and forgiveness that she taught him ultimately led to the peace treaty between Anwar Sadat and Menachem Begin at Camp David. Think about it: Millions of people in Egypt and Israel were saved from war because of what a little old Sunday school teacher did in Plains, Georgia, fifty years ago. I think that is worth repeating: Millions of people were saved from war because of a Sunday school teacher! She was "living large" and beyond herself without even knowing it.

To realize that you may never know the effect you are having on the world by your simple good deeds—doesn't that just send shivers up your spine?

It makes me sober and humble as I consider who may be observing my behavior—and how I might be influencing them. It should prompt us to seriously reconsider our commitment to God and love and how we live out our commitment in the church and our communities, neighborhoods, and workplaces. How will what we do today affect the souls of thousands tomorrow?

To Christians, this advice may seem familiar and not very profound. The challenge for us is to change from a casual "head knowledge" and mental assent to these principles and adopt a deeper level of action. Neurotics must intentionally make service to others a priority. And this servant attitude must come from a conscious, heartfelt choice not driven by neurotic compulsion.

How do we achieve this? The answer is old—ancient, in fact—and comes from the Christian tradition of the monastic orders.

The monastic enclaves of the Middle Ages are often overlooked wells of wisdom. When we say the word *monk*, most folks get a mental picture of a lone, crazy, bearded hermit hiding away on a remote mountain. Such monks were the exception, not the rule. The monastic orders were, by and large, not filled with introverts but rather were groups of Christians who wanted to discover what it means to live the good life in a truly Christian setting. They had no desire to escape from social interaction—they simply sought to establish a utopian community where the teachings of Christ, particularly the concept of loving our neighbors as ourselves, could be fully lived out. Of course, their definition of "good life" and "utopia" were the antithesis of the modern usage of these terms. From the eighteenth century on, most efforts at utopia were aimed at personal hedonism, seeking the easy life, the pleasure palace, the life free of trouble. All such efforts failed, reminding us that the origin of the word *utopia* comes from two Greek root words that literally mean "no place." The monks failed at creating utopian paradises, but they did succeed in finding ways of living that embody the ideals of Christian love and that purposefully seek spiritual maturity.

Some of their strategies for great living included maintaining spiritual disciplines (prayer, private scripture reading and study, public worship), being employed in meaningful work, deferring to others in gentle kindness, finding times for silence and stillness, journaling, and communal interaction with an eye to always helping the weak. All of these "strategies" used by the monks are relevant for our times. Consider them the dues you must pay to become a mature person and a worthy teacher. But please take note that if we attempt to make Christian maturity a personal achievement rather than a work of God, we have missed the whole point! This is why the chief goal of the monastics was to seek humility.

When one of the church fathers was asked to define humility, he replied, "Humility is a great work and a work of God. . . . [It means to] suffer injury and endure. . .scorn and injury and loss with patience."[1]

Humility, like love, is a choice and a discipline that

we alone can make—but the power that enables us to attain humility comes from God. True humility is God's work. True humility never says, "Look what I have achieved!" Thus the monastics repeatedly cautioned against religious pride: "If an angel appears to you, do not accept it as a matter of course, but humble yourself and say: 'I live in my sin and am not worthy to see an angel.' The devil appeared to a monk in the guise of an angel of light, who said to him: 'See whether you were not sent to someone else. I am not worthy that an angel should be sent to me.' And the devil vanished."[2]

The path of humility is not wide or easy. The path to humility narrows to a tightrope, strung tautly between immorality on one side and prideful, guilt-driven duty on the other. If the monks, who had each other to help them on their walk, had difficulty walking this tightrope, how much more challenging for you and me! Most of us cannot dwell behind the walls of a religious conclave. We live, rightly, in our dark cities, bland suburbs, and provincial hamlets, trying to find both happiness and purpose in the varied company of strangers and friends. And in our postmodern age, we watch helplessly as our society swings back and forth between austere Victorianism and pornographic indulgence, between fundamentalist pharisaism and unmoored, libertine subjectivity.

Good people, neurotics especially, are plagued with an outsized sense of duty, yet we find no joy in fulfilling those guilt-driven obligations. We must find the narrow middle way. Again we can benefit from the writings of

W. E. Sangster: "'Duty' as the keystone of ethics leaves much to be desired. It is somber, straining, and straitened. It freezes the genial current of the soul. It catechizes every simple pleasure [and] rations laughter. . . . Right at its heart there is holy egoism—because its own rectitude is the aim and not the adoration of God or the love of one's neighbor. Self sits enthroned. . .a self in sackcloth and ashes, an immolating and macerating self—but still self."[3]

Were Sangster still alive, I might share royalties with him, because I find myself in such agreement that I continue to quote from his wisdom. As the saying goes, I could not have said it better myself, so I won't try. "Our passionate devotion to 'duty' as the means to holiness may be a disguise for exhibitionism. . . . The men who have most given themselves to the slavish observance of duty—Stoics, Pharisees, ascetic monks, and Puritans—are, for the most part, hard and cheerless souls. They seem to be quarried, not born. They are not *happy*, and the flaw is fatal. They do not recognize joy as a necessary mark of the saint."[4]

Pursuit of self-righteousness and pious perfection is doomed to failure because it almost always focuses on *self*. Oswald Chambers, author of the classic call to piety, *My Utmost for his Highest*, warns us of how the search for personal sainthood can backfire. He wrote, "Beware of an abandonment which has the commercial spirit in it—'I am going to give myself to God because I want to be delivered from sin, because I want to be made holy.'"[5] Anything that is all about the unholy trinity of "I, me, and mine," should make us cautious.

I have grown suspicious of the much-repeated phrase "a personal relationship with Jesus Christ." We need a *communal* relationship with Jesus Christ. We need the zeal of the monk and the Pharisee but the heart of Christ, who did not die just for "me," but who died for an entire world. The apostle Paul reminds us that "Christ died for the ungodly" (Romans 5:6). Jesus even died for my enemies! One of the last words Jesus spoke to His disciples was an instruction to go and tell the world. The gospel was not their private property. And Christ's last word, in the book of Revelation, was not meant just for John but for "the churches." Revelation 3:20, one of the few verses in which Jesus alludes to anything like a "personal relationship" ("If anyone hears my voice and opens the door, I will come in and eat with him, and he with me") was addressed to the whole *ekklesia*, the "gathering of the community." Jesus does not want us to retreat in pious isolation or to wallow in dutiful shame. Sangster concludes, "Love has a keener vision than duty. It notices things. It could not tolerate the [constant] neglect of dear ones which the most dutiful men [are guilty of]. The fruit of goodness is not found by lopping off healthy branches of the tree of life or exalting asceticism to the skies. Hating oneself can become as obsessional as hating another. The way forward is to let love crowd sin out."[6]

Neurotics and modern-day Pharisees are still busy lopping off their limbs. Guilt-ridden, they have taken literally and seriously something that I believe Jesus intended as a joke. Jesus said in Matthew 5:30, "And if your right hand causes you to sin, cut it off and throw it away." We have no record of any one-handed followers in the early church. I believe that is not because they were sinless, but because they were present when Jesus said those words and they heard Him laugh! What He was doing in the Sermon on the Mount was, by hyperbolic humor, showing the absurdity of the Pharisees' attempts at moral perfection and asceticism.

In essence, Jesus was saying, "If you claim to be so perfect, pluck out your eye so you won't accidentally lust after a pretty woman." He would have been horrified if anyone had actually done so. That kind of perfection is not the aim of kingdom living in this world.

It is wiser to fill up on goodness than to try to clean out our badness. This is the principle that Jesus taught in His parable about the fellow who got rid of one demon only to be filled by more (they saw the VACANCY sign!). To live beyond ourselves means to joyfully engage the wider community, to love our neighbors, and to be more concerned with caring for the needy than about whether we appear holy and pure on the outside.

The point bears repeating: To live the life I'm describing calls for true humility. Humility cannot be grasped. It must be lived. Humility is love embodied. The humble person wears love like a garment. A rough analogy is when weak, mild-mannered Clark Kent puts on his Superman costume. He becomes something far greater than a timid newspaper reporter—as Superman, he goes out boldly to save the world.

As a child, I looked a lot more like Clark Kent than I did Superman. I even wore the black horn-rimmed glasses. My neurosis manifested in shyness and outright fear. I trembled at the thought of speaking in public (interestingly, I became a preacher), and only once did I make myself the group's center of attention. Here's what happened: At a Halloween party as a seven-year-old, I began to perform a "striptease." That's right, I began to take off my clothes! You can imagine the horrified looks on the faces of the adult chaperones as they considered how best to stop me. I had been dressed in a black suit and tie—what had seemed like a strange Halloween costume, I'm sure—but now I was removing it, along with my horn-rimmed glasses, to reveal that I was actually *Superman*! Yes, a neighbor had given me a very well-made Superman outfit, cape and all, and I was excited to find that it fit me and made a wonderful Halloween costume. The chaperones sighed in relief, and all my friends commented on what a cool costume I had. For one evening, at least, I had become Superman.

My childhood neurosis also manifested in terrible nightmares. In my dreams, monsters would chase me and horrible dark things would happen to me. The answer to my fear came in a strange trick exercised by my subconscious mind: In one nightmare, my dream-self suddenly realized that I was—underneath my street clothes—actually Superman. Once I became the costumed Superman, my dream-self was no longer afraid of anything or anybody. Amazingly my mind was able to repeat this trick. The nightmares ceased.

Sigmund Freud might have had a field day interpreting those dreams, but for me, the message is simple: We all have within ourselves the ability to choose a bigger, better self. The superperson within us has been placed there by God. Indeed, Genesis tells us that we were made in the very image of God! That divinely planted seed of greatness has been marred and obscured by sin, neurosis, and no-telling-what-else, but it is still within us.

When we fully adopt the persona of humility and love, we become a Superman or Superwoman. Interestingly, the Latin origin of the word *super* means "above" or "superior," whereas the origin of *humble* is "humus," meaning "low as dirt." Humble Christians make no claims to superiority; rather, as Jesus said, we are to "be the very last, and the servant of all" (Mark 9:35). But Jesus also goes on to say, "The last will be first." Paradox is the hallmark of Christianity!

When we begin to live beyond ourselves, when we kill our narcissistic egos and begin living for others, we become new creatures—dare I say *better* creatures! The closer we get to becoming what God originally created us to be—humble, loving, sharing, caring people—the more we reclaim our heritage as beings made in the very image of God Almighty.

We began by saying that "God is love." Living beyond ourselves means becoming more and more a creature of love. That is a powerful thing—*the* most powerful thing. Love trumps all the other cards. Love will triumph over

Pharisees and N-types, judgmentalism and hate. Love is mightier than swords and gunpowder because it conquers without harming anyone. Love is invulnerable, even to kryptonite!

Love is always at hand, waiting for us to choose it. Love is the one thing eternal in our present position—all other things will go the way of rust and dust. As the Beatles sang, "All you need is love." As the apostle Paul said, Love is the greatest of all things.

And God is love. So give me God, love, and maybe some chocolate, and I will live beyond myself. How about you?

~~~

Notes

1. *Sayings of the Fathers in Western Asceticism* (Philadelphia: Westminster Press, 1958), 173.

2. Ibid., 171.

3. W. E. Sangster, *Path to Perfection* (Nashville: Abingdon-Cokesbury, 1943), 153–54.

4. Ibid., 154.

5. Oswald Chambers, *My Utmost for His Highest* (New York: Dodd, Mead, 1935), March 12 devotional.

6. Sangster, *Path to Perfection*, 155.